A Taste of the Country

JIMMY DOHERTY

A Taste of the Country

Photography by **Chris Terry**

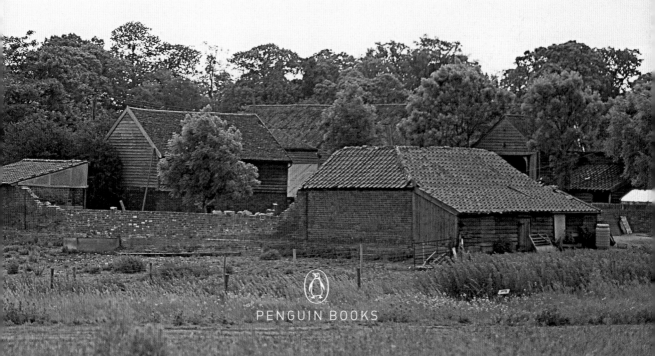

PENGUIN BOOKS

Dedicated to the beautiful Michaela

Published by the Penguin Group

Penguin Books Ltd, 80 Strand, London WC2R 0RL, England

Penguin Group (USA) Inc., 375 Hudson Street, New York, New York 10014, USA

Penguin Group (Canada), 90 Eglinton Avenue East, Suite 700, Toronto, Ontario, Canada M4P 2Y3 (a division of Pearson Penguin Canada Inc.)

Penguin Ireland, 25 St Stephen's Green, Dublin 2, Ireland (a division of Penguin Books Ltd)

Penguin Group (Australia), 250 Camberwell Road, Camberwell, Victoria 3124, Australia (a division of Pearson Australia Group Pty Ltd)

Penguin Books India Pvt Ltd, 11 Community Centre, Panchsheel Park, New Delhi – 110 017, India

Penguin Group (NZ), 67 Apollo Drive, Rosedale, North Shore 0632, New Zealand (a division of Pearson New Zealand Ltd)

Penguin Books (South Africa) (Pty) Ltd, 24 Sturdee Avenue, Rosebank, Johannesburg 2196, South Africa

Penguin Books Ltd, Registered Offices: 80 Strand, London WC2R 0RL, England

www.penguin.com

First published by Michael Joseph 2006
Published in Penguin Books 2007
1

Printed in Italy by Printer Trento s.r.l

ISBN: 978-0-141-02674-9

ABOUT THE AUTHOR

Jimmy Doherty was born in the beautiful Essex countryside, and has been passionate about nature and farming for as long as he can remember. After leaving school, he became an entomologist at Molehill Wildlife Park, the Natural History Museum and Coventry University, but in 2003 he decided to leave the study of insects behind him to set up a rare-breed pig farm in Suffolk. His trials and tribulations were filmed by the BBC and he wrote his first book, *On the Farm*, to accompany the series. He still lives and works on the farm with his girlfriend, 300 or so pigs, 4 cows, 15 sheep, 2 dogs, 2 cats, 100 chickens and too many foxes.

Contents

- Introduction 6
- On the Farm 14
- In the Wild 78
- The Great Outdoors 144
- In the Garden 190
- In the Kitchen 254
- Useful Addresses 314
- Index 316

Introduction

Two years ago I embarked on an adventure of a lifetime. My plan was to start and run my own farm, producing free-range, rare-breed pork of the highest quality. The pigs would run wild-free through an ancient, shaded woodland and would be sold through a traditional farm shop situated in a crumbling cattle barn. The only problem was that I had no real 'official' training in farming and the farm had been derelict for the past fifteen years. To say things were absurdly difficult would be an understatement.

When times were hard they were desperately hard, but with a passion for good, honest food and a burning desire to return to a life of simple pleasures, I somehow kept going. I know now, with hindsight, that to really follow your dreams you must have a firm belief in your planned project along with optimism and a good sense of humour. I was also blessed with the love of my wonderful girl, Michaela. The struggles have been lightened by her presence here on the farm and her support in my darkest hour has helped me to push onwards and upwards. One question I'm always asked, however, is how did I find myself running a farm in the first place?

In one way or another the seeds were sown very early on in my life. As far back as I can remember I have always been fascinated by the natural world around me. It can be as grand as gazing up at the canopy of a massive old oak, or as simple as watching a spider crawl across the leaf of a pot plant. This fascination often got me into trouble at school, as rather than paying attention to what was happening on the blackboard I was either staring out of the window or drawing pictures of animals in the back of my textbooks. However, it was at school that my boyhood passion for nature really began to take shape. My first day at secondary school was mind-blowing. I was introduced to new subjects such as geography, biology and geology, which I had heard of but didn't really know much about. I wasn't the best student in the world,

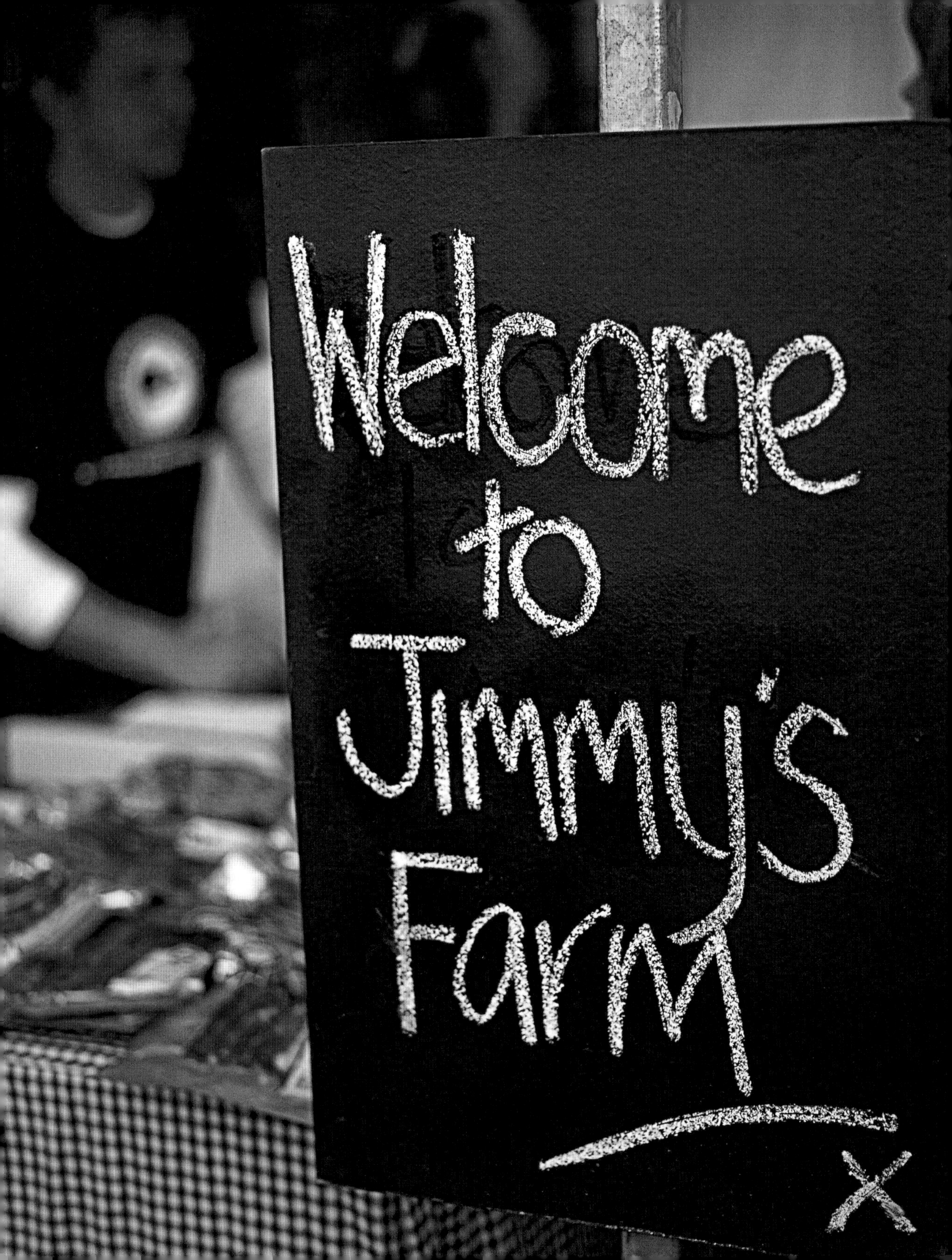
Welcome
to
Jimmy's
Farm
x

but I couldn't get enough of this stream of knowledge and information. Suddenly the natural world around me, which had for so long been the focus of my attentions, was slowly being explained. It was as though somebody had suddenly turned a light on. I am afraid some subjects, such as French and German, passed me by, much to my regret, but the natural sciences really indulged my imagination. We were lectured on subjects such as dinosaurs and volcanoes, the formation of continents, how rivers shaped the landscape, the relationships between animals and plants, and the workings of the human body. This was just music to my ears!

At the age of thirteen most of my friends had weekend jobs that ranged from paper rounds to washing cars, the most hated of chores. I, on the other hand, was extremely lucky because my mother had happened to come across an advert in the local paper advertising a vacancy at Mole Hall Wildlife Park in Essex. The job was for a young weekend worker to help with general duties of animal care. This would be a double hit, as not only would I be earning money (£1.13 an hour), I would also be working with animals. It was my first job interview – I was thirteen years old and desperately scared. However, the angst buried deep in my stomach was swiftly replaced by a profound sense of embarrassment, because my mother insisted not only on attending the entire interview but on answering in full many of the questions for me before I could open my mouth. I felt a bit like Ronnie Corbett in Sorry!. But to my mother's credit, she must have done a good job, as I was asked to start the following weekend.

I thought I had hit the big time. I was surrounded by exotic birds, monkeys, chimpanzees and a whole host of other weird and wonderful creatures. This was just the beginning – I truly believed I had died and gone to heaven. The lady who owned this marvellous menagerie was Mrs Pamela Johnstone. Despite being in her senior years, she had great determination and spirit, a wonderful woman, the type of character people would have once called a true 'Brit'. She had spent her life travelling the world studying wildlife, and promoting conservation both at home and abroad. Mrs Johnstone was one of the people who has had a great effect on my life, and I still hold her dear to my heart. She inspired me not only to travel but to also further my passion academically.

Like most lads my age I had a big group of mates, and one of my best friends was Simon Day. We used to spend most of our time at each other's houses, driving our mothers crazy as we rushed about leaving disaster in our wake. It was during the time I spent at Simon's house that I learnt about traditional rare-breeds, because Simon's father, Colin, (another of my childhood heroes) used to farm rare-breed cattle and sheep. Colin taught me the importance of preserving these creatures as part of our living heritage, as well as introducing me to some of the best meat I have ever tasted. He's the main reason I know about domestic rare-breeds. One spring evening after school I stayed over at Simon's house for dinner (probably unannounced). I remember we all had to keep getting up to check their Ryeland sheep, as lambing was in full swing. That evening I watched the birth of one of Colin's first lambs, which the family called Buttons. We all gathered around to watch this tiny little white creature struggle to its feet. I can still feel the anticipation and the following joy once the lamb began to suckle from its mother. From that point on, I thought, this is for me!

I followed my passion for all things natural, completing a degree in zoology, and then went on to study for a PhD in ecological entomology. My grandfather use to tease me about my extended education, saying, 'By the time you finish school it will be time for you to collect your OAP bus pass.' It was during my PhD that I suddenly found myself facing a fundamental, life-changing moment. Academic study had for me drained the colour and excitement out of the natural world that had once intoxicated me as a child. Ironically, the more I tried to get closer by understanding more about the subject I loved, the further away I felt. My average day was spent in the basement lab of Coventry University, sitting at a microscope, identifying and counting flies. I became more and more despondent about my research, and felt a real need to get back to a life where I could be happy and contented. I thought to myself, I need more

out of my life than a microscope and a small pile of flies! It was time for a change. I began to think more and more about my childhood days spent working at the wildlife park and those times helping out on Colin's smallholding with his cows and sheep. I had always loved the idea of producing my own food and being self-sufficient – I had read the books of John Seymour, and was already baking my own bread and growing a few vegetables on a tiny bit of ground at the back of my student garden. This was fine, but I wanted to go the whole hog, to live out my dream of running my own farm, producing my own produce.

However, it was a big step from growing a small patch of lettuces to running a working farm. It would of course have to work as a business – pay the bills and wages as well as supporting Michaela and myself. Although my heart was filled with images of the good life, I realized immediately that this was not a game or a flight of fancy. Before I could go out and buy a pair of wellies, some research was needed. Where was I going to sell all the sausages and bacon I would be producing? At that time the papers were full of stories of farmers going out of business, and people leaving the land, news which began to put doubts into my mind. I needed some reassurance that it could work. I was convinced that there were people out there who would be prepared to pay a little more for traditional quality food with real flavour.

My reassurance came in the form of a man called Peter Gott, one of Britain's real food legends. I first heard of Peter through a friend of mine who regularly bought bacon from him at Borough Market. He told me I should go down to the market and see Peter, as he would be very interested to meet me and could probably point me in the right direction. My friend had told Peter what I wanted to do and that I would be dropping by the market to see him for a chat. Peter was easy to spot – he's a large character with a broad Cumbrian accent, and wears a brown bowler hat, a red neckerchief, a waistcoat, and a pair of plus-fours complete with knee-high red socks. I introduced myself to him and just as we shook hands Peter said to me, 'If you want to make a million pounds from farming start with two.' Then he let out a roar of laughter! He took me to his stall and explained the different cuts of meat and the variety of sausages he had on offer. After my tour Peter suggested I should spend a few days at his farm, so that I'd understand how he manages to turn free-range pigs into profit. The time I spent at Sillfield Farm was invaluable. I began to see that cutting out the middleman and selling direct to the public was a viable and reasonable option.

After this crash course I was most definitely hooked, and Peter agreed to help me find a farm of my own and give a hand in getting me started. This selflessness is a reflection of his passion for British farming and traditional food production, and I can never thank him enough for all his kindness over the years. After finding a farm we were off on our journey, and since then we have faced fire and flood, and everything in between. The farm is now up and running, with a busy farm shop and butchery selling fantastic pork, beef and lamb as well as a whole range of homemade sausages and bacon. We still have a long way to go, but we are finally living the life that Michaela and I both dreamt about. For me, achieving my own little bit of the good life is a way of escaping the rat race, even if it is just for a few hours. Reaching that good life is what this book is all about. I have written it so that there is something for everyone. I didn't want it to be solely aimed at people who want to start a smallholding, I wanted it to offer a slice of the good life to a wider audience. Not everyone has the time or space to grow their own vegetables, but you will find that this book has a relevance regardless of whether you live in a city flat or a country mansion. I want everyone to feel the simple pleasures of life that we often neglect in our modern world, whether it's keeping chickens or growing a few herbs on your window ledge – it's all there just waiting to be enjoyed!

On the Farm

On the whole British farming has been in desperate decline in recent years, mainly because consumers are not prepared to pay a realistic price for their food, and because of the middleman taking all the profit. Those farmers who seem to be succeeding are the small-scale specialized producers who sell direct to the consumer. However, other types of farming and commercial enterprise are on the increase, ranging from running a self-sufficient smallholding to keeping chickens and growing a few veggies in the back garden. Despite the scale, and whether it's part-time or full-time, in my eyes it's still farming because it's all about producing food, and there are now specialized papers and magazines covering every imaginable subject, from herb-growing to goat-keeping. People want a piece of the good life – they want to have a go for themselves and produce food they can trust.

Compared to most of the farms in my area mine is on a relatively small scale, although I must say that with 300 pigs, six cows, fifteen sheep, four goats and some 200 mixed poultry, as well as ten beehives, it doesn't always feel like it. It makes me feel tired just going through the list. On the whole, the animals I keep are traditional rare-breeds. At Pannington Hall we farm in a very traditional way: the pigs forage in the woodlands and the chickens scratch around in the fields and farmyard. So it makes sense to stick to traditional breeds of farm animal.

Such breeds are often the animals of yesteryear that went out of fashion because they didn't fit with modern intensive methods of farming and food production. The reasons why these beautiful animals have become rare in our modern farming landscape are the very reasons why I chose to farm them. First they have the ability to put down a decent amount of fat, which not only aids cooking but results in the flavour of the meat being out of this world

(I must say I had never tasted real crackling until I roasted a joint from one of our own pigs). If you are worried about too much fat in your diet you can always cut it off once it has played its part in the cooking. When people see fat on a joint of meat or bacon from a traditional breed, they feel they are being cheated, because it looks as though they are getting less meat for their money compared to well-presented ultra-lean supermarket meat. But think how often you've bought a joint of meat or a pack of bacon in the supermarket only to find that when cooked it resulted either in a dry tasteless lump, due to the absence of natural fat, or a watery mess in the frying pan, due to the addition of water (added water makes the packet heavier – equivalent to the old trick of the butcher's thumb on the scales). I love cooking real bacon where the fat turns crispy and the meat doesn't shrink – just think how much you are being ripped off when most of your bacon is evaporating as water vapour.

Another reason why traditional breeds fell out of favour is that they can't be hurried, by which I mean that they are slow-growing, or rather grow naturally and don't suit intensive systems of production. Muscles take time to grow properly, and an animal that grows naturally will have better-developed muscles and will produce well-structured meat with a greatly superior texture. However, slower-growing animals cost more to feed as they are around longer, and the meat will inevitably be more expensive. This is fine as long as the consumer is prepared to pay for it. Traditional breeds of farm animal have been developed over many years to suit their environment, with the ability to forage for their food and be naturally hardy in our climate.

There is also a personal reason why I keep rare-breeds, and it's because I feel a real sense of pride that in this country we possess such a diversity of livestock. They are part of our culture and national heritage, an agricultural gift that we have given to the world. Wherever you travel you are likely to see breeds of domestic livestock that have their origins in our islands. It's a shame we don't make more of a song and dance about them; if this was Italy or Spain we would be singing their praises from the treetops, and there would be government funds to help save them!

All the animals on the farm have a role to play, whether it's producing pork, or eggs, or helping to maintain the land. For example, I use my goats and Soay sheep to keep down the rough pasture and scrub. I get immense pleasure from working with the animals too – it's food for the soul! To achieve your own piece of the good life doesn't mean you have to take such a drastic plunge as I did, it doesn't even mean that you have to keep chickens or grow your own vegetables. It's all to do with scale, and you can achieve a part of the good life in many ways – making your own sausages, or just shopping in the knowledge that the meat you buy has come from an animal that has not been reared intensively, but has been allowed to roam free-range and fed on an appropriate diet.

This chapter focuses on farm animals – not necessarily the ins and outs of their husbandry (after all, not everyone is going to start keeping pigs), but more what to look for when buying pork, or making the most of your roast chicken. One of the most important links I want to stress is the one that exists between the animals we farm and the food we produce. Only when we understand this relationship can we really begin to appreciate our food, not only for its taste and flavour but also for the tradition and heritage enshrined in its production. We should feel a sense of pride when we eat food traditionally produced in our country – for me it's a bit like watching Britain getting a gold at the Olympics.

Pork

The key to good pork is how the pig has lived, and this includes where it lived, what it ate, and how it was treated. In my opinion you should only buy pork that has been reared in the open air – after all, would you eat lamb that had never seen a grassy field? Keeping pigs outside is important for two reasons, first the welfare of the animal, and second the quality and flavour of the meat, which is a world apart from that of intensively reared indoor pigs. I've studied and worked with animals all my life, from chimps to butterflies, and I must say pigs are among the most intelligent animals I have ever come across. I would rank their intelligence alongside, if not above, that of dogs.

My experiences with pigs have taught me that they are highly social creatures with complex behaviour and deep-rooted instincts. They also have the ability to form relationships with one another: for example, I have two Tamworth pigs that love to be together; if they are separated into different enclosures, with other pigs that they have known just as long, you'll find both of them together in the same pen next morning. To deny a pig the opportunity to display its natural behaviour to a reasonable extent is out and out physical and psychological cruelty. Pigs that are reared intensively inside specially designed sheds are often so overcrowded that their freedom of movement is restricted. Some indoor pig systems do not even allow straw on the floor of their enclosures, but opt for bare concrete or slats so the muck drops through. Such conditions prevent the pig performing one of its most natural activities, rooting around in the ground – it's almost like denying a child the opportunity to play or laugh.

Being confined in such a way leads to displays of unnatural behaviour, comparable, I imagine, to the rocking motion common in people who have spent their whole life locked up in a cell. For pigs, such behaviour can take the form of tail-chewing – a pig will turn its attention to the tail of another and begin to chew on it, causing discomfort and serious injury to its victim. The farmer's answer to this is not to give the animals more space or to enrich their environment, but rather to clip the pigs' tails when they are young. The overcrowded conditions are also responsible for numerous fights between individuals. In a normal situation, where pigs have freedom to roam, fights are rare, as it is less likely that an animal's personal space will be invaded. When a fight does break out, the loser will flee to a safe area and the whole thing will be over in seconds. However, where animals are confined so that they cannot help but intrude on each other's space, fights are commonplace, and as there is no real room for the defeated animal to retreat to, such fights can result in death.

It's not surprising that a pig that has had a poor quality of life will produce poorly flavoured pork. Pork in the supermarket, the outlet for most intensively reared indoor pigs, bears no resemblance to what I would call real pork. The meat is often wet, lacking the pigment and structure of pork from an animal that has been allowed to exercise properly and lead a stress-free existence.

Intensive pig farming, like intensive chicken farming, has resulted in super hybrids – animals that have been selectively bred to grow much faster on less food in a much shorter time than their traditional cousins. This is due to the remit given to the farmer via the supermarket being quantity rather than quality. Indeed, the trade-off for such speedy growth over such a short time has been loss of flavour and reduced animal welfare. Added to this, the farmer is under continued pressure to produce pigs with less and less fat. It may sound good to have less fat, but you lose all the flavour of the pork. The super-lean pork chops you see on the supermarket shelves have no real taste of porkiness and dry out very quickly compared to a chop from an animal that has a bit of fat on it. Such pressure (due to the consumer wanting more lean than fat for less money without realizing the cost to the animal) has resulted in the development of commercial hybrid pigs that have the ability to put down only the minimum amount of fat. I know, because I once kept two such pigs with a group of my traditional breeds that were being fattened for slaughter. All were given the same food – but it didn't matter how much the commercial pigs ate, they did not put on fat. When all the pigs were killed, the traditional rare-breeds had a fantastic layer of snowy white fat, whereas the super-pigs had less than a centimetre.

Real Flavour

The pork I produce is from pigs that lead a completely free-range life, roaming over pasture and woodland where they are free to root for wild foods such as chestnuts, acorns, roots, tubers and mushrooms, as well as any beetle grubs they may come across. The resulting meat is deep in colour and well-structured, with fat marbling throughout. Once cooked, the pork is packed with amazing rich nutty flavours, and due to the marbling the meat remains succulent and juicy on carving. Such a culinary wonder has little to do with cooking and everything to do with the raw materials, i.e. the animal. The food the pig eats enriches the flavour, natural exercise develops the muscles, and the rate of development of the animal is also very important – the slower the better! My pigs can take almost twice as long to reach slaughter weight as their indoor intensively reared counterparts. A slow-maturing animal will not only have well-structured muscles, but will have excellent fat marbling through the meat in comparison to an intensively reared fast-maturing pig.

I keep lots of pure traditional pigs such as the Essex, but from time to time I mate my sows with a male pig that has lots of wild boar blood in him. This has the effect on the resulting piglets of slower growth, and most pig farmers would view it as madness and see me as going backwards rather than forwards because the pigs will take longer to produce, costing more money to feed. However, I feel I am not going backwards if my goal is quality rather than quantity, and slow growth is so important in achieving this. A recent visit to Italy proved this – I found that farmers with similar pigs to mine were doing exactly the same thing to produce hams that rank among the best in the world. They have found that the fat from pigs allowed to mature naturally in free-range systems changes in its properties. As the pig develops, the fat alters from saturated to unsaturated, so from a naturally reared slow-growing pig you are not only getting fantastic-tasting pork, but it will also be healthier to eat. It all makes sense really! Things that are left natural can only be better for you; when you rush and cut corners something has to give.

Buying Meat

Rearing a couple of pigs at the bottom of the garden is very rewarding but much more involved than, say, keeping a few hens. There is lots of mucking out, greater cost in fencing and a lot of paperwork, as you will need a holding number, a herd number and movement licences. If you have the time, the space and a head for red tape, go for it – you will never look back. However, if you are not in a position to keep your own pigs, where do you buy real pork? It isn't straightforward at first, as you won't find it in a supermarket, but with a little research you will be rewarded with some of the best pork you have ever eaten in your life! Your first port of call should be your local farmers' market or butcher. At the farmers' market you can talk to the farmer first hand and ask how he rears his animals, what breed they are and where they are killed. At a butcher's shop it's a little trickier, because you're dealing with the middleman, but a really good butcher will know exactly where and how his meat was reared and will be more than happy to accommodate your queries. Think about it, if a butcher has got some of the best meat around in his shop he is not going to keep quiet about it, is he! However, if he's reluctant to answer your questions and doesn't really know where his meat has come from or how it was farmed, I think you have wasted enough of your time and should shop elsewhere.

Once you have found a good butcher, stick with him – it's a relationship that will last for years, and in some cases for generations. If you want to buy good-quality, locally produced meat you must start supporting you local butcher's shop. It's not just about meat, it's also part of keeping our tradition alive and our communities thriving. If you are lucky enough to have a butcher's shop near you that is accredited by the Traditional Breeds Meat Marketing scheme, a wing of the Rare Breeds Survival Trust, or better still a member of the Guild of Q Butchers, you can be assured that the meat on offer will be from producers of a certain standard who farm traditional breeds naturally. Farm shops are another outlet where you can buy quality pork sausages and bacon that will either have been produced on the farm or sourced locally for their quality. If there isn't a farmers' market or decent butcher's shop in your area, there is another option to explore, especially if your time is at a premium. The internet has now become a vital tool for many farmers and producers in getting their produce direct to the consumer, and it's a real way in which they can compete with supermarkets. I can understand why people opt for the convenience of a supermarket over regularly shopping at a farmers' market if they work unsociable hours, or don't have the means to travel to a farm shop. What I don't understand are those people who shop online from a supermarket for all their needs when buying direct from the farmer is only a couple of clicks away. You don't have to get into your car, or spend time walking round the market (although I think everybody should!), so there would appear to be no excuse for not buying direct from the producer. If you think about it in this respect, we have never had it so convenient when it comes to buying quality food in this country, so let's take advantage of the times in which we live.

Common cuts of pork

Loin

I think the loin is one of the best cuts from the pig. It's from the middle back of the animal and is often cut into smaller joints that are usually boned and rolled, such as the fore loin, middle loin and chump end. The loin with the bone in makes an excellent roast or can be cut for pork chops. On the loin is a thick strip of meat that runs along the underneath of the backbone – this is the tenderloin or pork fillet. The tenderloin, as its name would suggest, is the most tender and leanest part of the animal, which makes it great for quick cooking. I like to butterfly it and pan-fry it with garlic and fennel.

Belly

It you love crackling this is the cut for you. The belly can be roasted either rolled, which gives the opportunity for stuffing it with herbs such as rosemary and thyme, or laid flat, allowing faster cooking. This was one of my favourite cuts as a student, because it's one of the cheapest, due to its fattiness, but there's no compromise on flavour. If you roast it flat, make sure you score the skin well and rub in salt, garlic and a small amount of chilli for a crackling bonanza! When buying pork belly it may be offered with the ribs still in – these can easily be removed with a boning knife and cooked as spare ribs. If you don't fancy removing the ribs yourself, get your butcher to do it for you.

Shoulder

I prefer a shoulder joint to a leg when it comes to roasting. A boned and rolled shoulder makes a great slow-roasting joint – the meat is tender, sweet and packed with flavour. Choose a joint with a decent amount of fat to keep the meat moist while cooking, and score the skin well beforehand for great crackling.

Leg

One of the classic Sunday roasts, the leg is usually boned and rolled and cut to form small roasting joints. Compared to other cuts of pork it's much leaner, and this is where the traditional breeds come in: the fat is essential, otherwise the meat will become too dry, so make sure your joint has enough fat to carry it through the cooking. Cook slow and long, but power up the heat at the end to crisp the skin. Leg of pork is cured to produce hams and gammon joints.

Hock and trotter

Not many people eat trotters or hocks these days, which is a great shame because the trotters make great brawn and the hock has masses of meat on it. Trotters often end up in the bin in most butcher's shops, and hocks are often cured to make bacon hocks or boned out and put into sausages. However, in our shop we have adapted an Italian recipe that turns both the hock and the trotter into a delicacy we call stockman's hock. We keep the trotter attached to the hock but cut off the toes for a more appetizing appearance. Then the bone of the hock is removed. This is done by cutting down one side of the hock until the bone is exposed, and the flesh is then cut away from around the bone until it comes free. The cavity is seasoned, stuffed with sausagemeat and sewn up with string, then the skin is scored and rubbed with rosemary, garlic and lemon thyme. The whole joint is put into a hot oven and roasted for around an hour, until the skin crisps up. Once rested, it can be carved into beautiful slices with a sausagemeat centre. There is always a fight for the trotter, with its delicious crispy skin that just screams to be eaten with your fingers.

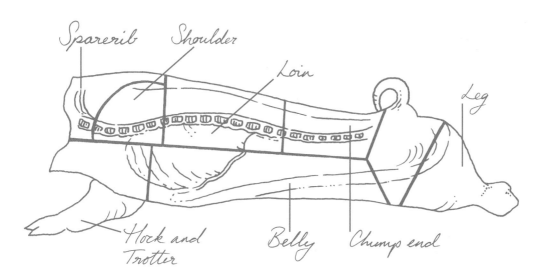

Toad-in-the-Hole

The sight of a massive dish of piping hot toad-in-the-hole arriving at the dinner table brings childhood memories flooding back. I remember the anticipation as a large helping was dished up on my plate and gravy slowly drizzled over while I sat with knife and fork at the ready! A real English classic.

Serves 4

- equal quantities each of plain flour, milk and eggs (you will need a measuring jug)
- pinch of salt
- freshly ground black pepper
- 8 Suffolk farmhouse sausages
- optional: a little oil
- 2 tablespoons beef dripping or white vegetable fat

Preheat the oven to 200°C/400°F/gas mark 6.

To make the batter, fill the jug up to the half-pint or 300ml mark with flour. Sift into a large bowl and add salt and freshly ground black pepper.

Break eggs into the jug up to the half-pint or 300ml mark (you'll need about 6, depending on their size). Make a well in the centre of the flour, add the eggs, and gradually beat them into the flour using a wooden spoon. Measure out half a pint or 300ml of milk and slowly beat into the mixture until the batter is the consistency of double cream. Strain through a sieve, pushing through any remaining lumps. Cover and leave to stand for 30 minutes.

Heat a large non-stick pan and cook the sausages over a medium heat until golden brown all over. If you don't have a non-stick pan, add a little oil. Set aside.

Place the dripping or vegetable fat into an ovenproof dish and pop the dish into the oven for 5 minutes or until the dripping is hot and hazy. Add the sausages to the hot dish and pour in the batter. Immediately return the dish to the oven and cook for 35 to 40 minutes, until well-risen and golden.

Serve the toad-in-the-hole with baked beans, onion gravy, mushy peas . . . or whatever takes your fancy!

Sausages and Ham with Red Cabbage

Serves 4

- 1.5kg/3½lb red cabbage, very finely chopped
- 115g/4oz gammon rashers, cut into 2.5cm/1 in strips
- 30g/1oz butter
- 300ml/½ pint stock
- 2 apples, e.g. Cox's, peeled, cored and diced
- 2 teaspoons caster sugar
- 1 teaspoon salt
- ¼ teaspoon white pepper
- 450g/1lb sausages (good herby ones work well)

This is an old Suffolk recipe that dates back to 1823, and it's a great supper dish, even 183 years later! I love dishes like this – simple, honest and full of real flavour. What else could you possibly need apart from seconds?

Preheat the oven to 160°C/300°F/gas mark 2.

Put the cabbage into a casserole with all the rest of the ingredients except the sausages. Bring to the boil, then cover tightly and cook in the preheated oven for 3 hours.

Remove from the oven and stir well, checking the seasoning. Most of the stock should have been absorbed. Keep the cabbage warm while you fry or grill the sausages.

Heap the cabbage on a serving dish and arrange the sausages on top.

Roast Pork

Leg and loin are the prime cuts of pork for roasting, either on or off
the bone, but a roast shoulder of pork is my favourite. It's slightly fattier
than the other cuts, and I cook it a little more slowly so that the fat
renders down, melting through the flesh and giving a lovely moist,
sweet, tender result.

Serves 4–6

• 1.7 kg/3 ¾ lb boned pork shoulder   • sea salt

Preheat the oven to 230°C/450°F/gas mark 8.

To ensure perfect crackling, score the rind and fat about 5mm/¼ inch apart but
without cutting through to the meat. Put the meat in a colander over the sink and
pour boiling water over it – this helps open the score marks so that the fat can
bubble through. Rub the dry, scored skin with sea salt, working it thoroughly into
the score marks.

Put the meat on a rack in a roasting tin and cook in the preheated oven for
15 minutes. Reduce the heat to 180°C/350°F/gas mark 4 and cook for a further
1¾ hours.

Remove the pork from the oven and leave it to rest in a warm place for at least
15 minutes – this allows the juices that have bubbled out of the meat to settle.

To carve, remove the crackling first.

Pork Scratchings

There's nothing like sitting in an old pub with a good pint of beer and munching some really decent pork scratchings – they have to be the classic pub snack. Here's a basic method for making fantastic homemade scratchings, but you can make them as elaborate as you like – try adding some chilli or fennel seeds.

Ask any butcher and he will gladly give you some spare pork skin, preferably with a little fat left on it. Scald it with boiling water and roast it in the oven at 230°C/450°F/gas mark 8 until crisp, golden and brittle. Any excess fat from the underside can be scraped off if you don't like it.

Leave to cool, then break up into small pieces. Season with salt and freshly ground black pepper – great served with drinks!

Rillettes of Pork

I first learnt about this from my French mate Raphael when we were housemates at university. After visiting his folks back in France he would often return with a box full of goodies, one of which would always be a jar of rillettes. Since then I have been addicted to the stuff, and secretly I think it's one of the reasons I keep pigs. If you are into charcuterie you must give this a go!

Serves 4

- 1 tablespoon rendered pork fat or lard
- 450g/1lb boned rare-breed belly pork, rind off and diced
- ½ teaspoon ground allspice
- ¼ teaspoon grated nutmeg
- 2 cloves of garlic, peeled and crushed
- ½ teaspoon salt
- a sprig of fresh lemon thyme
- 3 tablespoons wine or water

Preheat the oven to 140°C/275°F/gas mark 1.

In an ovenproof pan, melt the fat and add the pork, allspice and nutmeg. Put the pan into the oven – the cooking time will be around 3 hours in total and you should stir the mixture frequently to prevent it sticking.

After 2 hours, add the garlic, salt and lemon thyme, adding a little wine or water if the mixture looks dry. The meat should cook gently without browning.

The meat is cooked when it is soft enough to shred easily with a couple of forks – pull it apart into loose fibres.

Baked Ham

Christmas would not be Christmas without a baked ham – the smell alone just shouts jingle bells! A traditional cured ham is not only a taste sensation but is part of our food heritage, and at one time every region would have had its own particular cure and method. Sadly most of these have died out in favour of commercial methods; however, there are still a few producers going strong, and believe me it is well worth seeking one out.

Check the weight of the gammon and calculate the cooking time, allowing 20 minutes per 450g/1lb plus 20 minutes. A 1.8kg/4lb gammon joint will take around 1 hour 40 minutes. Place it in a large pan and cover it with cold water. Bring slowly to the boil and drain.

Return the gammon to the pan, add the vegetables, bay leaf and peppercorns, cover with cold water and bring slowly to the boil. Skim any froth off the surface with a slotted spoon. Cover the pan and boil gently for half the cooking time (in this case 50 minutes). Meanwhile preheat the oven to 180°C/350°F/gas mark 4.

Drain the gammon and wrap it in foil. Place it in a baking tin and bake at 180°C/350°F/gas mark 4 until 15 minutes before cooking time is completed. Remove from the oven and increase the oven heat to 220°C/425°F/gas mark 7.

Remove the foil and strip the rind from the gammon, leaving the fat on the joint. Score the fat in a diamond pattern and stud with cloves. Sprinkle the surface with demerara sugar and pat it in.

Bake in the hot oven for the remaining 15 minutes until crisp and golden. Let the joint sit and rest for at least 15 minutes before carving. Serve hot or cold.

Serves 8–10

- 1.8kg/4lb middle gammon joint
- 1 large onion, skinned and quartered
- 2 medium carrots, thickly sliced
- 1 bay leaf
- 6 black peppercorns
- cloves and demerara sugar to decorate

Lamb

You can't really go wrong with lamb that has been reared in this country, and it is tastiest in late spring and early summer when the grass is at its best. The UK is blessed with weather and an environment well suited to growing the lush grass that helps produce some of the best lamb in the world. Sheep farming has escaped the intensification that has plagued the egg, poultry, pork and dairy industries, mainly due to the fact that sheep are easily raised on land that is either impoverished or marginal, at little expense.

We have just started to keep sheep on the farm – they have real charm, and each animal has its own distinct character. We run two different breeds, the Jacob and the Soay, each producing very different meat. The Jacob is a more conventional lamb-producing breed, although the sheep look very distinctive with their brown and white fleece and curved horns. The other breed, the Soay, is from a group of sheep breeds known as primitive, i.e. less domesticated. These sheep produce lamb that has a much smaller carcass than most other breeds but is more intense in flavour. I love the fact that there is this distinction between my sheep. However, one thing both breeds have in common is their lack of respect for my fencing or for anything I have to say, or shout, to them. As a result they please themselves around the farm. I have given up trying to chase them back into their field, but they seem happy enough to stick around, and farm life carries on as usual.

Britain has such diversity, both in breeds of sheep and in natural environment, and we produce very distinctive lamb as a result. For example, there are the Downland breeds, raised on calcareous (chalky) grasslands, hill breeds such as the Herdwicks, which roam the hills of the Lake District, and the Welsh mountain sheep that forage for mountain grasses and herbs. Which has to be Wales's second most famous export – after Tom Jones. We even have sheep that feed on the salt marshes, giving the meat a distinct and delicate flavour.

Many of the production systems such as hill grazing would be awarded distinct regional certification if performed on the Continent and command high prices. However, in this country there is no distinction: prices are kept low by cheap foreign imports, and all the British-produced lamb you buy in the supermarkets is lumped together – what a waste. The best way to taste selected breeds from the distinct regional areas is to buy either direct from the farm gate or via a farm's web page. Another option is your local butcher or farmers' market.

Lamb needs to be hung before it's eaten, to mature and tenderize the meat. The ideal is meat that has been hung for a least a week, but for lamb to be matured for this length of time it's essential to have a good layer of fat. If you buy extremely lean lamb and the butcher tells you he has hung it for a week, he isn't telling you the truth. So far I have just talked about lamb from sheep that have been matured to the age of about six months. Any animal that is taken on past its first year is classified as either a hogget (which is a sheep over one year old – often primitive breeds such as the Soay are used as they are slower-growing than most) or mutton, which is an animal two years old. This type of meat is hard to find, and you will only be able to source it from certain butchers and farmers' markets, but it will be well worth your trouble. If you ever find mutton dressed up as lamb, consider yourself lucky! The meat will need longer hanging but the flavour you get from a mature animal that has fully developed its muscle structure will be something you won't forget.

Common cuts of lamb

Leg

The classic leg of lamb is one of the most popular joints for roasting in this country. Taken from the hindquarters, it's one of the most expensive cuts, and can be bought whole or as smaller joints, both on the bone or boned and rolled. Either way it's great roasted with loads of rosemary and garlic.

Shoulder

I much prefer the shoulder to the leg – it has more fat covering and I find the meat sweeter. The shoulder is from the forequarter of the animal and is often broken into smaller joints, again either on the bone or boned and rolled.

Saddle

The saddle is basically the back of the animal, taken from a carcass that has not been cut in half. Once split, the saddle forms two loins. The whole saddle forms a huge roasting joint, great for parties if you have the means to cook such a big piece of meat. You can buy smaller cuts from the saddle which form a much more manageable joint for roasting. Small sections are often cut to form Barnsley chops, which are basic chops that have not been divided.

Loin

The loin (the saddle split in half) has a good eye of lean meat and may be bought either with the bone in, when it can be cut to give you classic lamb chops, or boned and rolled. Either way the loin makes an excellent roast.

Breast

The breast is the lamb equivalent of pork belly and is best boned and rolled to form a small joint. You get a lot of flavour for your money, because it's one of the cheapest joints. It's quite fatty, so it lends itself to slow roasting or stewing.

Neck

The Neck forms several cuts. The best end of neck joins on to the loin and forms an excellent joint; chops are often taken from the best end of neck to form cutlets. Neck fillet is the middle of the neck once it has been boned – the meat is tender and is good grilled or fried. Middle neck is a very bony section between the best end and the scrag, and is often sold separately or with the scrag attached. Despite having a lot of bone in proportion to the meat, the flavour is wonderful and is fantastic stewed or used in a broth or soup. Then there is the scrag which I think is a horrible name for a great piece of lamb that adds real flavour and substance to any stew or curry.

Scrag · Middle neck · Best end of neck · Loin · Chump · Leg · Shoulder · Breast

Liver and Bacon

My Nan Vi would always make this for my grandad – it's simple but so tasty. You hear many people today banging on about Italian and Spanish peasant food and how wonderfully rustic it is – well, you can't get any more rustic than good old British liver and bacon.

Serves 4

• 750g/1lb 10oz lamb's liver

• seasoned flour

• 12 rashers of dry-cured streaky bacon

• oil for frying

Wash the liver briefly, then pat dry with kitchen paper and slice thinly (about 1cm/ $1/2$ inch thick), removing any coarse tubes. Dust the liver in the seasoned flour.

Heat a large non-stick frying pan and add the bacon. Fry until crisp and golden, then remove from the pan, drain on kitchen paper and keep warm. There will be bacon fat left in the pan.

Add the liver to the pan and fry for a couple of minutes on each side – it cooks very quickly and overcooked liver can be dry and tough, so take care!

Serve with mashed root vegetables and cabbage.

Shepherd's Pie

Like many busy working mums, my mum couldn't always pick me up from school because she often had to work late, so a lovely lady from the village called Ann would collect me twice a week and look after me. She would give me home-baked goodies and cream soda, but the real treat came at supper: Ann would bring out her shepherd's pie. It had a fantastic crispy potato thatch over delicious mince, carrots and onions. It remains one of my favourite dishes today, even though I can never make it exactly as lovely old Ann did.

Serves 4 generously

- 450g/1lb minced lamb
- 2 onions, chopped
- 2 cloves of garlic
- 2 level tablespoons plain flour
- 2 carrots, peeled and chopped finely
- 1 x 400g/14oz can of chopped tomatoes
- 1 level tablespoon tomato purée
- 115ml/4fl oz beef stock
- 1 tablespoon Worcestershire sauce

For the topping

- 1kg/2lb 3oz floury potatoes, peeled and chopped
- 5 tablespoons hot milk
- 30g/1oz butter
- salt and freshly ground black pepper
- 50g/2oz Lancashire or any crumbly cheese

Dry-fry the lamb with the onions and garlic for 8 to 10 minutes or until well browned. Stir in the flour. Add the remaining ingredients and season to taste. Bring to the boil, then cover and simmer for 30 to 40 minutes.

Meanwhile make the topping: cook the potatoes in boiling water until tender, then drain well and mash, stirring in the hot milk, butter and seasoning.

Preheat the oven to 200°C/400°F/gas mark 6. Pour the lamb mixture into a 1.7 litre/3 pint shallow ovenproof dish. Spoon the mash over the meat and sprinkle with the cheese.

Bake in the preheated oven for 20 to 30 minutes, until piping hot and golden brown.

Squab Pie

I've always thought squab pie contained young pigeon, which are known as squabs. In the original regional recipes I have come across, however, it has always been made with lamb. In most regions apples and spices are included, and in Devon, in particular, they add prunes and it's served with clotted cream!

Serves 4

- 225g/8oz plain flour
- 50g/2oz butter, diced
- 50g/2oz lard, diced
- 675g/1½lb lean lamb neck fillets, sliced
- 1 large cooking apple, peeled, cored and sliced
- 450g/1lb onions, thinly sliced
- 8 ready-to-eat prunes (optional)
- ¼ teaspoon ground allspice
- ¼ teaspoon grated nutmeg
- salt and freshly ground black pepper
- 150ml/¼ pint lamb or beef stock
- milk to glaze

Preheat the oven to 200°C/400°F/gas mark 6.

Sieve the flour into a large bowl and rub in the butter and lard until the mixture looks like fine breadcrumbs. Add just enough water to form a firm dough. Knead lightly until smooth, then wrap in clingfilm and chill until required.

Lay half the lamb slices in an ovenproof pie dish (about 900ml/1½ pint size).

Cover with half the apple, onions and prunes (if using), and sprinkle with the allspice, nutmeg, salt and freshly ground black pepper. Repeat the layers, then pour over the stock.

Roll out the pastry on a floured surface so that it is big enough to fit the pie dish. Cover the dish, moistening the edges to create a seal. Brush the top with milk and bake in the preheated oven for 20 minutes.

Reduce the temperature to 180°C/350°F/gas mark 4, and bake for a further 1 hour 15 minutes, checking occasionally to see that the pastry does not get too brown. If necessary, cover with tinfoil.

Traditional Gravy

Gravy is a great comfort food. As it's poured over your meal it fills the air with its luscious smell, giving a real feeling of homeliness, especially when it's raining outside. This is a basic method that uses all the lovely sticky bits left in the roasting tin after a roast or after frying in a pan.

Makes about 450ml/ ¾ pint

Pour off excess fat from the pan, leaving about 2 tablespoons. Sprinkle in about 2 tablespoons of plain flour and stir over a medium heat until rich brown in colour, scraping up all the bits stuck to the bottom of the pan.

Add 450ml/ ¾ pint of hot stock and cook until thickened, stirring all the while. Season to taste.

You can, of course, add whatever takes your fancy . . . a handful of fresh herbs, softened, sweet brown onions, wine or ale in place of some of the stock, a dollop of redcurrant sauce, good for lamb . . . the list is limited only by your imagination!

Lancashire Hotpot

This is another fantastic regional dish that we as a nation should celebrate – it really is the best of British. There are lots of variations on this traditional recipe, some using lamb cutlets, the most traditional including oysters. This is my simple version.

Serves 6

- 675g/1½lb middle neck of lamb, trimmed and cut into cubes
- 2 tablespoons seasoned flour
- 2 tablespoons oil for frying
- 450g/1lb potatoes, peeled and sliced in rounds
- 2 onions, sliced
- 3 carrots, peeled and sliced
- salt and freshly ground black pepper
- 300ml/½ pint lamb or beef stock
- butter

Preheat the oven to 190°C/375°F/gas mark 5.

Toss the lamb in the seasoned flour and fry in the hot oil until brown. You will need to do this in batches. In a large casserole dish, place alternate layers of vegetables and lamb, seasoning each layer and ending with a layer of potatoes. Pour over the stock.

Dot butter all over the potatoes, then cover the casserole and bake for 1½ hours.

Remove from the oven, take the lid off the casserole, and brush the potatoes with more melted butter. Return to the oven for another 30 minutes, uncovered, to brown the potatoes.

Beef

A lot of people complain about the weather in this country, saying we have terrible summers. If it's a regular suntan that you are after, you may be right, but if you're talking about beef production we have the best weather in the world. Our mild, slightly wet climate creates a fantastic environment for growing the lush grass which is the raw material for any decent beef. The other essential raw material needed to create one of this nation's favourite meats is obviously the cow, a noble animal that is a master at converting grass into meat. The UK is responsible for the majority of the beef breeds in the world, and you will find British breeds of cattle being farmed in the USA, Argentina, Australia, France, Germany, Italy, Russia . . . in fact you name it and they will be there. That's more than you can say about any other British industry. I don't see many Americans driving around in British-designed cars, but lots of them eat beef from Aberdeen Angus cows. And where does most of the beef we eat in this country come from? A lot of it is now imported, believe it or not, especially if you eat at any of the well-known fast-food chains.

However, to discuss most of the beef you are likely to come across that has been farmed in this country I have begun with milk production. You may think this very strange, and might ask yourself what the milk you find on the supermarket shelves has to do with the beef joint a few aisles down. The answer is that you would not get one without the other, because the dairy industry is the main producer of calves destined to be reared as beef. But this raises the question: if we have such fantastic beef breeds, why do we rely on the offspring of cows that have been specifically bred for milk, not beef? Like any other mammal, including ourselves, for a dairy cow (the black and white Friesians that are commonly seen out of the car window as we whiz down the motorway) to start the process of milk production she has be pregnant. Every year, each dairy cow has to have a calf to keep her producing milk, and this will carry on until she needs replacing as she comes to the end of her productive life. The farmer will only

need to replace her with a new cow about every eight years, so what happens to all the calves born within that time? The answer is that they go into the beef industry. However, the pure-bred dairy cow is not designed to convert grass to good-quality beef, but concentrates on converting all her food into producing milk. As a result, most farmers choose a beef bull to act as the sire of the calves rather than a dairy breed. The resulting calves are a cross between a dairy and a beef breed, and such crosses are responsible for the majority of beef produced in the UK.

If these animals are given good conditions and are well fed on a natural diet they will produce acceptable beef. However, due to financial pressures on the farmer to produce beef cheaper and faster, such cattle are often fed high-protein concentrates to fatten them quickly, resulting in meat that, I feel, lacks the flavour of beef produced from a slow-growing, grass-fed, traditional beef breed. Producing beef more naturally will be less cost-effective for the farmer unless we, as the consumer, begin to demand higher quality, and at the same time accept that we have to pay a fair price for such a product. We have to start putting our money where our mouths are, stop blaming farmers and start examining how we as a nation shop. We need to consider what our priorities are when it comes to spending our money.

For real top-quality beef you need to look to those farmers who specialize in beef breeds. Such herds are known as suckler herds, and many are based on traditional British pedigree breeds. If you are lucky enough to buy meat from one of our traditional breeds your tastebuds will be in for a gastronomic journey they will never forget! I remember the first time I ever tasted such beef: I was about fourteen and I'd been invited by my mate Simon Day to his house for Sunday lunch. Simon's dad, Colin, despite working in the City, also ran a fair-sized holding which included Ryeland sheep, Rhode Island Red chickens and a herd of Dexter cattle. Nowadays he also breeds some of the best Gloucester cattle in the country. Colin had a big effect on my life as I grew up, because he introduced me to real food production, and in many ways was almost a second father. He's probably the main reason why I now run a farm myself. Simon's dad had recently had one of his Dexters killed and Rosemary, Simon's mum, had roasted a joint of the beef in the Aga for lunch. Until that point all the beef that I had ever eaten was from the supermarket. When the roast appeared on the table it was dark in colour, with a wonderful covering of yellow creamy fat, and once sliced it revealed the fantastically marbled tender juicy pink meat. The texture was like butter and the flavour was deep and lingered on the palate – I felt as if I could have eaten the whole cow! You are not likely to find such meat at the supermarket, but you will find it at your local farmers' market or quality butcher, and you can often buy it direct either from the farm gate or on the internet. When you are buying your beef, look out for the Rare Breeds Survival Trust accreditation or ask the farmer or butcher what breed the beef has come from.

Most common cuts of beef

Forerib

There has recently been a resurgence in the popularity of this joint – it appears regularly in food magazines, its praises sung by a choir of celebrity chefs. There is a good reason for this cut of beef stealing the limelight, because it makes one of the most fantastic roasts around and represents everything that's great about our islands. It is a large roasting joint, taken from the back of the animal between the wing and the back ribs. You can either roast it on the bone, which helps to keep in the moisture when cooking, or have it boned and rolled. Either way this joint is best cooked slowly.

Sirloin

This is a large joint that contains the fillet and is cut from the back of the animal. I like it best cooked on the bone – I feel it retains more moisture that way, and has better flavour – but you can also buy it boned, with or without the fillet. A number of different steaks are cut from the sirloin: sirloin steak, cut from the top end, fillet steak, taken from the undercut, and T-bone steak, which is cut between 25 and 60mm thick and contains the characteristic T-shaped bone that gives it its name. All these steaks are great fried or grilled, while the sirloin joint itself is best medium-roasted.

Rump

This is cut from the top of the back end of the animal just before the tail, to form rump steak. This steak is my favourite – although it's not as tender as other steaks, it has bags of flavour. It's great simply fried. You may also come across a cut known as top rump, which is cut from a lower portion of the hindquarters. This is a fairly lean cut with a close grain that is best pot-roasted.

Topside

This is a lean boneless joint taken from the hindquarters – it has no natural fat covering but will be sold with a layer of beef fat tied round it. Always make sure this layer of fat is generous, and cook it slowly, otherwise the meat will dry out and become tough.

Silverside

Silverside is similar to topside and adjoins the top rump. It makes a boneless roasting joint with a close-grained texture. It should be treated like topside, in that it will require a good layer of fat and a slow low-temperature roast to get the best results.

Shin

Muscles that have done a lot of work during an animal's life will have the best flavour, but they will also be the toughest. Both these conditions are perfectly illustrated by the shin, which is the lower section of the cow's foreleg. It is packed with flavour, but to make the meat tender it needs to be stewed or casseroled slowly for a long time but it is well worth the wait.

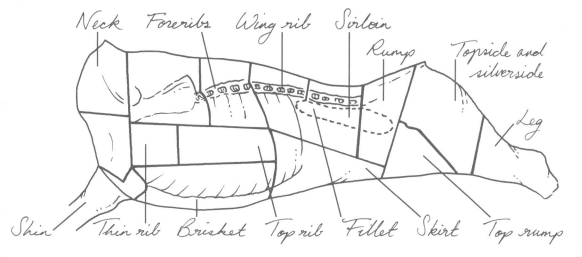

Boiled Beef and Carrots

All my grandparents were from the East End of London, and they had a song about boiled beef and carrots which, when I was a child, sounded like some sort of torture. I think it was more to do with their singing voices than with the food. It was only later in life that I discovered what all the song and dance was about. It's a great way to make the most of the cheaper cuts of beef and is a real working-class classic, celebrated all over the world in many variations.

Serves 6

- 1.5kg/3½lb lean salted silverside or brisket of beef
- 2 small onions
- 8 cloves
- 1 bouquet garni
- 6 black peppercorns, crushed
- 18 small carrots

Soak the meat in cold water for several hours or overnight, then drain and rinse. Put it in a large saucepan, cover it with water and slowly bring to the boil. Pour off this liquid and add just enough fresh cold water to cover.

Cut the onions into quarters and stick a clove in each. Add these to the pan with the bouquet garni and crushed peppercorns.

Cover and simmer for about 2 hours. Add the carrots and simmer for another 30 to 40 minutes, until the carrots are tender.

Transfer the beef and carrots to a serving plate and keep warm. Skim the fat from the surface of the cooking liquid and strain. Boil the liquid to reduce, and transfer to a sauceboat or jug.

Serve the meat sliced, with the carrots on the side. It is traditionally served with boiled potatoes, its own liquor as the sauce, parsley as garnish and a strong English mustard. Any leftovers are great in sandwiches, garnished with gherkins!

All in One Can of Beer Stew

This is a lovely, easy recipe that you can prepare quickly and it will sit happily in the oven until you are ready to eat. You can vary the vegetables to your own taste, and also the type of beer you use – lager will make a lighter gravy than, say, stout, but they'll all produce a tasty result.

Serves 4

Preheat the oven to 160°C/300°F/gas mark 2.

- 2 tablespoons flour
- salt and freshly ground black pepper
- 1kg/2lb 3oz shin of beef, cubed
- oil
- 2 medium onions, peeled and sliced
- 1 clove of garlic, crushed
- 4 large carrots, chopped into chunks
- 3 medium leeks, cleaned and sliced into rings
- 4 medium parsnips, peeled and chopped into chunks
- 4 medium potatoes, peeled and quartered
- 1 x 440ml can beer
- 565ml/1 pint stock (use a good-quality stock cube if you don't have any fresh)
- a sprig of thyme
- 1 bay leaf

Get a clean plastic bag and put the flour, together with a good grind of salt and black pepper, into it. Add the meat and jiggle it all around so the meat is covered with the seasoned flour.

Take a large casserole and heat a couple of tablespoons of oil. Take a handful of the seasoned meat from the bag and fry quickly until brown all over. Remove and put on a plate. Repeat with the remaining meat until it is all browned and put to one side.

Then add the onions and the garlic to the casserole and cook for just a couple of minutes until they start to colour – adding a little more oil if necessary. Tip in all the other vegetables and give them a good stir to mix. Fry for a couple more minutes, then return the meat to the casserole. Stir it all up and add the beer and the stock. Give it another good stir, then pop in the thyme and the bay leaf. Bring to the boil and check for seasoning – add salt and freshly ground black pepper to taste. Put the lid on the casserole.

Put the casserole into the preheated oven and cook for at least 2½ hours. You can leave it longer if you wish – just turn the heat down and check periodically that it isn't getting dry. Add more liquid if necessary.

Enjoy with some lovely fresh greens and, of course, a can of beer to drink.

Chicken

I had just turned thirteen when I began to keep chickens. I bought two hens
and a cockerel from a friend at school called James Barron for three quid apiece.
I remember getting them home and building a small run round a shed that my
folks didn't need any more – well, they didn't once I put chickens into it! That
was often the case in our house: my dad would return home to find that ferrets
were living in the coal bunker, or that a pond had appeared in the middle of the
garden. It's only when I look back that I realize how accommodating my parents
were. I used to let my hens free-range all over the garden, and more often than
not they would roost up in the high branches of the apple trees rather than
returning to their shed. This wild existence meant I had to go hunting for their
eggs in and around the bushes. I soon learnt the benefits of rounding the hens
up at the end of the day. There is one thing about keeping chickens that I'll never
forget, and that's the feeling of a freshly laid warm egg in my hand and the taste
once it was cooked, literally minutes later. It is an experience I think every child
should have.

Keeping chickens may seem expensive when you think about just popping down
the shops and buying half a dozen eggs, but try to think of the cost spread over
the chickens' productive life. There is no doubt that cost per egg from your own
birds will be slightly higher, but I think it's a small price to pay when you know
you are getting a supply of really fresh eggs from birds that are fed and kept the
way you want. But it's more than just eggs that you get from keeping chickens –
you get a real kick and satisfaction that money can't buy. Many people find it's
an excuse to get outside, spend time in the garden, and relieve the stresses
of modern living. An hour or two spent with the chickens has a relaxing and
therapeutic effect that takes you back to a simpler way of life. They make great
pets for kids, teaching responsibility at an early age and rewarding hard work
with fresh eggs, while at the same time instilling a knowledge of food

production. I also find that the odd hen scratching around while you turn over the veggie patch is a great companion, picking off the odd slug here and earwig there, all the while fertilizing the soil as she goes about her task.

Before you start keeping chickens you must ask yourself what you want them for. This may sound a bit stupid, but I think it's really important. Do you want your chickens just for eggs, or do you want them for meat, or both? What size of bird do you want, and do you care what they look like? These are all important questions, because your requirements will reflect the breed or type of chicken you end up keeping. However, there are no real hard and fast rules, and you shouldn't feel they are written in stone. If you choose a meat breed it doesn't mean it won't lay eggs, it just won't lay as many as a specialized egg layer. Once you start keeping chickens you will soon be under their spell, and you'll want to know more and more about them. After a while you'll wonder how you lived your life without them.

Where to buy chickens

I remember a friend who wanted to start keeping chickens saying, 'Where do you buy chickens from? You don't see them for sale in your local pet shop or garden centre.' Like most things, you need to know where to look. One way to track down a breeder of the type of chicken you want is to buy a specialist magazine, such as Country Smallholding or Practical Poultry, which will list chicken breeders and societies local to your area. Most local papers have a pets and livestock section in their ads pages, where you'll often see chickens advertised for sale. Buying chickens can be confusing – you'll find different age groups and funny terminology that may not make sense. Breeding stock are adults, point of lay (POL) are birds coming into their first laying season, and growers are young birds. The first two will start laying eggs almost immediately once they settle in and feel comfortable with their surroundings. Growers will probably not provide you with eggs until the following season, but they are a good way to start keeping poultry, and it's the way I started when I was a kid. I found I learnt a lot as the birds grew, and as they grew so did my confidence. If you are lucky enough to know someone who already keeps chickens, they may be persuaded to sell you a few hens – this is an excellent way to start your flock. You not only see the birds and know who you are buying them from, but you will be able to go to them for advice, a kind of after-sales service!

Housing and feeding chickens

You can quite easily keep chickens in any unused part of your garden or allotment, no matter how overgrown and weedy it is. (For the chickens it's all natural food.) If you have a fence around your garden you already have the makings of a chicken run, as the birds can easily be contained in one corner if you add a single fence to form a triangular run. If you have no desire for well-kept flowerbeds you can let them have the full range of your garden, but remember that they will scratch, dig and peck at most things green, so any plants you grow will have to be able to withstand their attentions. If you are going to fence your birds in, they will need either a run that is covered or a fence high enough to stop them hopping over. A six-foot-high fence will stop the most determined chicken. How beautiful you want your chicken enclosure to be depends on how handy you are, how much time you have, and how much money you want to spend.

Your chickens will need some form of shed to give them a dry and draught-free area to roost in, shelter from bad weather, and a place to lay their eggs. If you go to a DIY store you can buy a cheap shed which with a little adaptation can function quite well as a chicken-house. I was always terrible at building things: they would be perfectly functional, but would look like something from an episode of Steptoe and Son. You can buy excellent ready-made chicken-houses, with or without custom-made runs, which are not only functional but are also pleasing to the eye. The price you pay will depend on how many chickens you need to house and the features you require. For example, you can expect to pay around £300 for a hen-house and run which will accommodate six birds. This may sound a lot at first, but you must remember that it is a one-off payment and such a structure should last a lifetime if maintained well.

Dogs and cats

Cats only really pose a threat to small bantams or chicks, and I have found that once they have become acquainted, neither one is interested in the other's existence. Dogs, on the other hand, are different. If they grow up with chickens they get on very well with each other. However, if they are new to poultry they will take a little training. It's not that the dog wants to kill the bird, but it may wish to play or investigate. As dogs are easily excited and chickens easily frightened it will often lead to a response in the dog which, as I know from my experience with my dogs, Bracken and Cora, leads to the death or injury of the chicken. With a controlled introduction such problems are easily overcome, but never excite or try to catch your chickens in front of your dog if you doubt its behaviour around your poultry.

Foxes

Foxes are a real problem, and the only way to keep your chickens safe is to lock them up at night in their shed. If you are building a run that is static, make sure the wire is buried into the soil – this will prevent the fox squeezing underneath. If a fox does get into your chicken-house it will try to kill every chicken it can. This is because it wants to make the most of the opportunity. There are many theories of how to deter foxes, from leaving out socks filled with human hair to pouring human urine around the chicken-hutch. Such ideas are based on the theory that the fox will be deterred from attacking the chickens because of the presence of human odour. What a load of rubbish – if that were true there would be no such thing as the urban fox that inhabits our cities, which must reek of humans. As long as you keep your birds secure at night you should be fine.

Do you need a cockerel?

If you have a cockerel your hens will lay fertilized eggs – this has no effect on their eating quality but just means that if the hens decide to go broody (which means incubating their eggs until they hatch, which takes twenty-one days) you will end up with a brood of youngsters. You will have more hens, which means more eggs, but you will also have more cockerels. Too many cockerels in your flock will make life stressful for your hens and may affect their egg-laying. You have two realistic options: either sell your excess male birds with a couple of hens to start someone else up in chicken-keeping, or rear them to eat yourself. At first you may feel this is a hard thing to do, but if you want real food there is no better way of getting it than producing it yourself. I would rather eat a chicken I've raised myself, knowing that it has received my utmost care and attention in both feed and welfare, than an off-the-shelf supermarket bird that I have no knowledge of.

If you want to keep a cockerel and you have neighbours, pop round with a bottle of wine to discuss your plans, as they will be subject to an early morning alarm call. Don't forget to mention the bonus of free eggs for Sunday morning fry-ups! I have always kept a number of cockerels – I feel they complete the flock and maintain its natural order. The male birds are always trying to impress the hens, indicating food sources by clucking excitedly. They also keep the hens together and offer protection – many times I've been chased by a cockerel if he feels I am interfering with his girls. Apart from the practical side, cockerels are amazingly beautiful, and for me the farm wouldn't be a farm without them.

Buying chicken

If you are sickened by systematic cruelty, leading to premature death and the deformity of animals through overcrowding and inappropriate feed, the only chicken you should ever consider buying or eating anywhere should be free-range. If the chicken you buy in your local supermarket is not labelled free-range, I'm afraid you are personally responsible for terrible cruelty. All meat chickens that are not from a free-range system will be from the broiler industry. This also includes chickens that are turned into nuggets, and most takeaway chicken. Broiler production is a farming system that is perfectly legal under current legislation set down by the government, which suggests that the government is perfectly happy to let it continue.

Under the broiler production system (the normal production method of farming meat chickens in this country), the chickens are kept in large sheds containing 20,000 to 30,000 individuals, in some cases more. The birds are crammed into these sheds, so much so that one square metre has to provide room for nineteen chickens. If this were not bad enough, they are allowed only one hour of darkness a day. The reason most of these birds are kept under artificial lights for twenty-three hours a day is to keep them feeding. This is where these poor creatures spend their entire life, which now, with selected breeding (Frankenstein birds) and a mixture of antibiotics and super-feeds, lasts only forty-two days.

The evidence of such suffering can be found among chickens in a supermarket near you. Look for brown marks on the leg joints (hock or knee), easy to see when the legs are folded into the bird's cavity, though these marks are often cut off as they filter through the quality control process. How do these marks get on to the birds in the first place? As so many birds are crammed into such small sheds, a large quantity of chicken waste builds up. Bird droppings are very rich in ammonia, and as a result the chickens' feet and legs are chemically burnt by their own excreta. Next time you are in your local store, look out for such markings – if you see them, make sure you point it out to the manager and let him explain!

It is amusing to think how much of Parliament's time was taken up with the fox-hunting debate and that people marched through our streets on both sides of the fence. At the same time we allow the cruelty of the broiler system to continue without a single word raised. We seem to have our priorities mixed up – at least the fox gets to see the sky and feel the wind! However, there is some good news: this type of farming will stop if we stop buying chickens from the broiler industry. The power is in our pockets.

What to look for in a good chicken

Your local supermarket should stock free-range chickens – if not, you can source them through your local butcher, farmers' market, or even on the net. Getting your free-range bird through the post may sound strange, but they often deliver next day and you can buy your chicken direct from the producer, cutting out the middleman. This can only be good for the farmer and shorten the food chain. When selecting a chicken don't just concentrate on the breast, which should be ample but not over-excessive – look at the legs too. They should be well-formed and have darker flesh than the breast, the reason being that the leg muscles in a real free-range chicken will have done a lot of walking and there will be more myoglobin (the blood cells which carry oxygen to the muscles) present. I always prefer the leg to the breast – I find the dark meat on the bone has bags more flavour.

When choosing a bird for your roast, don't be worried if you see black stubble on its skin: these are just the remnants of coloured feathers. If you see such marking on chickens, always go for them, as it will be more than likely that you are buying a more traditional breed. Most commercial breeds are white in colour. The same is true with turkeys – at Christmas I always buy one that has got black feathers (try Kelly Turkeys in Essex for a real Christmas bird), such as the bronze or Norfolk black turkey. Be prepared to pay good money for a good chicken: a bird to feed four will cost you around ten quid, which is just about enough to cover the cost of giving that chicken a decent life. It's not a high price to pay when you think what we pay without question for other things in life, such as music CDs, going to the cinema, or a night down the pub. For the small price you pay you are getting not only peace of mind that your chicken has been reared naturally, but also the knowledge that it will also taste fantastic.

Chicken Sandwich

There is nothing quite like a really good chicken sandwich. It has to be one of my lunchtime favourites, and I really love to go to town with it. I think if you've got a good piece of free-range chicken, why not make the most of it? So here is my recipe for the best chicken sandwich, enough to serve two people because you won't want to share your own!

Preheat the oven to 200°C/400°F/gas mark 6.

Use a frying pan or griddle pan that can go into the oven, and get it very hot. Rub the chicken breasts with a little oil and season with salt and freshly ground black pepper. When the pan is hot, put in the chicken breasts, skin side down. Lower the heat and cook for 5 minutes, then turn the breasts over and cook for 5 minutes more.

In the meantime, put the tomatoes into an ovenproof dish, drizzle them with olive oil and season them with salt and pepper. Put both the pan containing the chicken and the dish with the tomatoes into the oven and bake for 15 minutes, or until the chicken is cooked through. Remove everything from the oven and leave to rest in a warm place.

Toast the bread and spread it with mayonnaise. Pile rocket leaves on top of two of the slices. Slice the chicken and arrange on top of the leaves. Spoon the roasted tomatoes over the top and finish with a dusting of freshly ground black pepper. Place the other pieces of toast on top to make the sandwich.

Keep a napkin to hand to mop up all the juices that you spill on your shirt!

Serves 2

- 2 free-range organic boneless chicken breasts, skin on
- a little olive oil
- salt and freshly ground black pepper
- 8 cherry tomatoes
- 4 slices of sourdough bread
- homemade mayonnaise (or a good shop-bought variety)
- rocket leaves

Spicy Chicken Supper

This is something I make to use up the drumsticks and wings of the bird. It's the ultimate finger food – fantastic for parties, barbecues, or as nibbles when you're settling down to a really good film.

Serves 2

- 2 chicken wings
- 2 chicken drumsticks

for the marinade

- 3 tablespoons runny English honey
- 3 tablespoons Worcestershire sauce
- 2 tablespoons spicy tomato sauce
- 1 chopped red chilli, to taste

Mix all the marinade ingredients together and toss the chicken pieces in it until completely covered. Leave in the fridge for at least 4 hours – and up to 24.

Preheat the oven to 190°C/375°F/gas mark 5. Shake the excess marinade from the chicken pieces and put the drumsticks into an ovenproof dish. Cook for 15 to 20 minutes, then add the wings and cook for another 15 to 20 minutes.

Check that the chicken is cooked right through, and serve with a crisp green salad.

Chicken Stock

Chicken stock is great to have in the fridge as one of your cooking essentials. You can use it to make soup, bolster gravy, or make a sumptuous risotto. This recipe uses up the leftover carcass, but I even save the bones from the plates once we have eaten the roast bird, as they really add to the richness of the stock ... nothing goes to waste.

Chop the vegetables into chunks. Put all the ingredients into a large pan and cover with water. Bring to the boil and skim off any scum that has formed. Cover and simmer very gently for 2 to 3 hours, then strain into a large bowl and allow to cool. Chill overnight, then remove any fat that has formed on the surface. Use within 3 days or freeze.

Makes about 2 litres/3½ pints

- 1 onion
- 1 carrot
- 2 sticks of celery
- 1 leek
- 1 chicken carcass
- 1 bay leaf
- 1 sprig of lemon thyme
- 2 litres/3½ pints water

Eggs

I think eggs are just amazing! Not only because they are a complete meal in their own right, but also because of their many structures, sizes and colours. Basically, an egg is a protective capsule containing everything a developing bird's embryo needs. Water is provided by the albumen or white, while the yolk acts as a protein-rich food reserve. Although eggs at first appear airtight, they are in fact porous, allowing oxygen in and carbon dioxide out. A decent egg should be fairly hard to crack – this shows that the bird laying it has eaten plenty of grit – and the yolk should be a good colour and sit proud of the white. When you taste a real free-range egg you never forget it. A lot of people think the colour of a chicken's egg will affect its flavour – do brown eggs taste better? Are white eggs better for baking? The answer is, colour doesn't matter. It's what the chicken has been fed on and how it has lived that make all the difference to the taste. It just so happens that different breeds of chicken lay differently coloured eggs. For example, Leghorns will lay pure white eggs, Welsummers' and Rhode Island Reds' eggs are dark brown, Light Sussex produce a buff-coloured version, Araucanas' eggs are a beautiful blue. Most breeds of chicken also come in miniature versions called bantams, which, as you would expect, produce smaller eggs.

Good-quality free-range eggs can be found at farmers' markets and most supermarkets. However, when buying eggs from a supermarket it can often be difficult to tell which eggs are from happy hens and which from those that have led a miserable life. Do you go for freedom-food-produced eggs, barn eggs, organic or free-range? They all sound fairly good, and often there is little to choose between the different methods of production. However, a name can be deceptive, so here are some descriptions of the types of egg production.

Conventional battery cages

This system is still legal and is responsible for 68 per cent of eggs sold in the UK. The battery system is basically an egg factory where the chickens' welfare has been massively compromised for economic gain. Five adult hens are kept in a cage measuring 50cm x 50cm (figures taken from the RSPCA) – that isn't even two feet square. The birds can barely move, let alone display any natural behaviour such as scratching for food. However, there would be little point in these poor animals doing that, as they are kept on wire mesh with no sawdust or chopped straw – please keep away from such eggs.

Enriched cages

This system is little better than the conventional battery cage. Enriched cages provide the birds with a little more room (we're talking centimetres here, not metres) and they have perches, a nest and an area to scratch around. The RSPCA state that such a cage system cannot properly provide these facilities for laying hens.

Barn eggs

Compared to cages, this system is much better for laying hens in terms of welfare – they have the freedom to move around and display most of their natural behaviour. Litter is provided to scratch around in, perches to roost on at night, and nest boxes for laying. However, barn eggs come from chickens that will only ever see the four walls of the barn. Such chickens do not have the liberty to range over open pasture.

Free range

In my opinion these are the only eggs you should buy. Here the hens are kept in buildings similar to the barn system but with one major difference – by day they are free to leave their quarters to roam and forage outside in the fresh air. In some cases, however, the area the birds are allowed to roam in may be limited. Nevertherless, if it does not say 'free range' on the label, don't buy them!

Other types of eggs available

Duck eggs

I must say that I prefer fried duck's eggs to chicken's – I find their richness delicious, although it's not to everyone's taste. Duck eggs have a bigger yolk, which makes them excellent for baking. They can be bought at most farm shops, in farmers' markets and even in supermarkets, but as with chickens, attention should always be given to the method of production. Duck eggs are usually blue or greenish, although buff and white eggs are not uncommon.

Goose eggs

Geese lay large white eggs with a very rich yolk but a somewhat watery white. They are ideal for baking, and make fantastic omelettes. Geese have a very short laying season compared to ducks or chickens, and their eggs are only really available from spring to midsummer. You can pick them up from your local farmers' market – they make a great Easter treat.

Quail eggs

Great things come in small packages, and this is certainly the case when it comes to quails' eggs. Not much bigger than a pigeon's egg, these beautiful cream and brown speckled delights are fantastic soft-boiled in salads. Again the quail has a relatively short laying season, so don't expect to see these eggs all year round.

Ostrich eggs

I love showing these eggs to my mates' young kids and watching their faces when I tell them that I've just found a dinosaur's egg! It's the largest egg produced by any living bird, and believe it or not they are available at a lot of farmers' markets, usually for under ten quid. In recent years ostrich farming has become popular in the UK, with a demand for the delicious lean meat, eggs, leather and feathers. These massive eggs make jumbo omelettes, as they contain 1.5 kilos of fluid.

Boiled Goose Egg with Chunky Soldiers

For a real Alice in Wonderland style breakfast nothing beats a huge goose egg, soft-boiled and served with well-buttered chunky soldiers. Geese have a short laying season, so their eggs will only be available from spring to midsummer. You will be able to find them at your local butcher's and farmers' market – although the price may seem expensive per egg, you get a lot for your money because each egg can weigh around 200g. When you serve a boiled goose egg to a child they may not be able to finish it, but it's hilarious just watching their reaction on being presented with such a big egg. The only problem you may have is finding an eggcup big enough!

1 goose egg per person

Place your goose eggs into a pan of boiling water and leave to boil for 20 minutes. Use a large pan with plenty of water to prevent the pan boiling dry and avoid the need for more water to be added. Once the eggs are boiled, put them to one side while you toast the bread. Cut slices from a fluffy country loaf and toast in your toaster, or if the slices are really chunky toast them under the grill, until golden brown. Butter well and cut into soldiers. Remove the top of the egg with a knife and serve immediately.

Spinach Omelette

I love omelettes! They are the perfect way of turning any left-overs into a spectacular dish, and when I was a student I soon found the benefit of always having a few spare eggs in the fridge.

Wash the spinach and put it into a sieve. Wilt it by pouring boiling water over it, then drain and leave to cool. Squeeze out the excess water and roughly chop.

Break the eggs into a bowl, add the water, season with salt and freshly ground black pepper and mix lightly with a fork.

Melt the butter in an omelette pan over a medium heat; when it foams, pour in the eggs. Tip the pan so that it is coated with the eggs, then, working quickly and using a fork, draw the cooked edges of the egg towards the middle of the pan so that the liquid egg runs underneath.

Once the omelette is almost set, add the spinach, the cheese and a grating of fresh nutmeg.

Using a spatula, fold the edge of the omelette over the centre third, then over again so that the fold is underneath. Tip on to a warm serving plate. Good with grilled tomatoes.

Serves 1

- a handful of young or baby spinach
- 2–3 eggs
- 1 tablespoon cold water
- salt and freshly ground black pepper
- 15g/½oz butter
- a handful of grated cheese
- freshly grated nutmeg

on the farm

Homemade Mayonnaise

Mayonnaise is one of those sauces that I always have to hand – it's great for making salad dressings, using as a spread in a sandwich, or for simply dipping your chips in!

Makes about 450ml/ ¾ pint

- 2 eggs, yolks only
- salt and white pepper
- 1 teaspoon Dijon mustard
- 2 tablespoons white wine vinegar
- 300ml/ ½ pint olive oil

Make sure all the ingredients are at room temperature.

Tip the egg yolks into a small bowl and beat them with a little salt and white pepper, the mustard and half the vinegar. Add the oil a drop at a time, whisking constantly to give a thick, glossy emulsion; you can start to add the oil in a thin stream once about a third of it has been incorporated.

Stir in the remaining vinegar and add more seasoning to taste.

Italian Warm Custard

My friend Gennaro taught me to make this classic recipe – it's known as zabaglione in Italy and sabayon in France but to me it will always be warm custard!

Serves 2

- 3 egg yolks
- 50g/2oz caster sugar
- 3 tablespoons sherry or marsala

Put the egg yolks and sugar into a bowl that will fit over a saucepan of simmering water (a bain-marie) and whisk until pale and frothy. The water should not be boiling. Slowly add the wine, whisking constantly. Turn the heat up under the pan, bring the water to the boil, and whisk until the sauce thickens.

Either serve at once, with poached seasonal fruit, or place the bowl of custard in a bowl of iced water, whisk until cooled, and serve cold.

Custard Sauce

This is my friend Nikki's famous custard sauce. She's completely nutty, but she does makes the best custard around.

Serves 4

- 565ml/1 pint hot milk
- 1 tablespoon caster sugar
- 2 eggs
- ½ teaspoon vanilla essence

Put the milk and sugar into a small pan and bring slowly to the boil. Remove from the heat. In a large bowl, beat the eggs. Pour the milk on to the eggs, stirring all the time to mix well. Return the mixture to the pan.

Place the pan over a gentle heat and stir constantly until the mixture thickens so that it coats the back of a spoon – this takes about 5 minutes, so be patient and don't let it boil! Pour the custard into a clean bowl, add the vanilla essence and stir.

Brown Bread Ice Cream

This is great because you don't need an ice-cream machine to make it. Having said that, if you do have one, you can use it for this recipe if you want. It's a fantastic way to get kids round the idea of eating brown bread.

Serves 6

- 85g/3oz brown breadcrumbs
- 85g/3oz soft dark brown sugar
- 2 large free-range eggs, separated
- ½ tablespoon dark rum
- 300ml/½ pint double cream
- 85g/3oz sifted icing sugar

Mix the breadcrumbs and brown sugar together and place on a grill tray lined with tinfoil. Grill under a moderate heat for 8 to 10 minutes, stirring frequently and taking care not to let the crumbs burn, until dark and caramelized. Leave to cool, then break up with a fork.

Whisk the egg whites until stiff. Mix the egg yolks with the rum and fold into the egg whites.

Whisk the cream and the icing sugar together until floppy and fold into the egg mixture along with the breadcrumbs.

Either churn in an ice-cream maker in accordance with your manufacturer's instructions, or pour into a shallow freezer container and freeze for 4 hours. Take it out of the freezer and put it into the fridge for 20 minutes before serving to let it soften slightly.

In the Wild

This chapter is all about peeking over the hedges and boundaries of the farm to see what delights lie beyond. It's about our countryside, our wildlife and the pleasure and food we can get from them. The woodlands, moors, rivers, lakes, beaches, hedgerows and fields of Britain support an incredible array of wild creatures and plants. The beauty of our landscape is there for everyone to enjoy. And, if you know where to look, you can take a little bit of nature home and cook up a fantastic feast for free.

The British countryside is an ancient landscape that has been shaped by the forces of nature for millions of years, and by human hands for thousands. This has created one of the most diverse and breathtaking places in the world. Most of our countryside didn't just happen, it's the shape it is for specific reasons. For example, hedgerows were planted by past generations of farmers to enclose livestock, and vast woodlands were cleared in order to open up areas for the growth of grass for grazing or to grow crops. As a nation we have been responsible for how our countryside looks today, but we are also responsible for how it will look in the future. In recent years intensive agriculture has changed our landscape drastically, with many hedgerows and woodlands being destroyed to form giant fields so that the equally giant machines that work the land will not be hindered. Such practices have a devastating effect on wildlife, destroying their habitats and food sources. Furthermore, over-use of pesticides and fertilizers has, in the past, caused them to leach into our streams and rivers, polluting the water and destroying the natural balance of life. Our countryside is continually under threat from modern farming methods and twenty-first-century living, and it is our responsibility as consumers to stop this destruction and safeguard the beauty of our countryside for generations to come.

Amateur Naturalists

All of us are born with an interest in the natural world – however, as we grow up this interest fades for many of us, due to a large extent to the pressures of modern life but perhaps also because it's something we associate with childhood and therefore discard as adults. A bit like playing with toys, I suppose. Others are lucky enough to keep this interest, which gives them excitement and stimulation throughout their life. I've found with many of my friends that underneath the serious grown-up surface still lives the excited child who is just waiting to get muddy. It does us good to get our toys out and play once in a while!

I can't remember a time when I have not been amazed by nature. It has always been a distraction in my life whenever I have had to conform to a working environment such as an office, or even at school. I was always the boy sitting by the window gazing at the world outside – there was always too much going on outside for me to pay proper attention inside. As a result my schoolwork suffered, which is plain to see when I read my old end-of-year reports. I used to be transfixed by the birds living out their daily dramas on the football field – in fact it was only those lessons that had a relevance for me, such as biology and geology, that were able to drag my gaze from the window.

My first memory of being mesmerized by nature is when I was five, when my family moved from east London to a small village called Clavering on the Essex–Cambridgeshire border. I might as well have been transported to the Amazon rainforest. The grey streets of London were replaced by green fields, the small back garden by a rambling wilderness of grass and flowers, the street lamps by apple trees. From that point on every day was an adventure with new treasures to discover, from newts and frogs in the pond to the brightly coloured butterflies flitting around the buddleia bush.

Hunter-gatherers

Before becoming farmers as we know them today, most of our distant ancestors would have been hunter-gatherers, sourcing food from the wilderness. As a nation, we no longer have to rely on the wilderness for our daily bread, but many wild foods are still in abundance and provide a natural larder for anyone prepared to take a walk on the wild side. Marginal habitats – hedgerows, field margins, woodlands – not only support the majority of our diverse wildlife, which includes anything from grasshoppers to fallow deer, but also provide a potential wild harvest. Collecting wild food is a great thing if it is done in the correct manner and with respect. Not only are you getting a natural feast, but you are out in the elements and walking in the countryside. You begin to see the hidden secrets of nature, and after a while you will be able to read and interpret them. You begin to see deer footprints in the wet mud, hear the alarm calls of birds, which may indicate the presence of an owl or sparrowhawk, and each time you will recognize more of the wild flowers and insects. I believe such abilities are within every one of us, because we haven't changed as a species for tens of thousands of years – all we need is a little refresher course.

This chapter forms the beginnings of that course. I would love more people to enjoy our wild landscapes, whether it's out in the depths of the countryside or in a city park (I've picked wild garlic in Hampstead and caught crayfish under a flyover in Coventry). The chapter will get you started on harvesting wild foods and making the most of natural resources. I have divided it up into seasons, to show you that whatever the time of year there will be something for you to pick, collect or make.

Where to Start Looking

If you are like me, you miss everything you set out to find but return with something you didn't expect, which is what it's all about. Each trip you make searching for wild foods will teach you more about where certain plants grow and thrive, or when a particular bush is going to come into fruit. The main places to avoid when collecting wild foods, especially plants, are roadside verges – first, because of the dangers of traffic, and second, because of the dust and contaminants belched out by passing cars. You should also avoid the edges of farm fields that have just been sprayed, as any wild plant you want to harvest will very likely have been sprayed as well.

The Countryside Code

These are basic rules that should be followed by anyone who wants to walk in the countryside, and in fact many of these rules should be followed regardless of whether you are in the country or the city.

1. Always take your rubbish with you – never drop it. There's nothing worse than walking in a beautiful part of our countryside only to come across a food wrapper. The other reason not to leave rubbish, and to pick it up when you come across it, is that it can harm, trap or even kill wildlife.

2. Protect plants and animals and keep your dog under control. Dogs can cause all sorts of problems for wildlife and farm animals, and keeping them on a lead will prevent any destruction or embarrassment.

3. Shut all gates behind you. You never know who is living in that field, and by leaving a gate open you could be responsible for the escape of livestock on to a road, or the untimely introduction of a bull into a herd of cows.

4. Don't start fires. Simply dropping a cigarette butt can start a very destructive wildfire in dry weather. Believe me – I have had some experience of how a fire can get out of hand, and once the wind is behind a grass fire it will spread faster than you can run!

5. Never trample across crops, or you will find yourself confronted by a very angry farmer. The crops are his living, and it's the equivalent of a bull in a china shop or walking over the fruit and vegetable display in a supermarket.

6. Never dig up and remove wild plants – this is essentially illegal. Also, if you remove a plant that could be used to provide you with wild food, you are killing the goose that lays the golden egg. Harvested properly and left where you found it, such a plant will reward you and others time and time again.

My Golden Rules for Collecting Wild Food

These are my personal rules to add to the countryside code on the previous page – I feel they are just as relevant when you are out collecting wild foods.

1. Plan your route and let people know where you are going and what time you expect to be back. See this as a form of travel insurance and peace of mind for you and your loved ones. Mobile phones can be a real nuisance but they are part of modern living, so take one with you. You never know when you might need one – you could twist an ankle or come across another walker who needs help. And if you want to change your plans, for instance decide after a long walk to stop at a country pub, you can call home and let them know you'll be a few pints late!

2. Only pick wild food that you are sure is edible, and never experiment by eating unknown plants on any occasion, especially out in the wilds on your own. If in doubt, leave it out!

3. Pick only what you need. There is no point finding an edible plant and stripping it. This will only mean wasted food and a dead plant, and you will have robbed other creatures of their share.

4. Take a friend with you. There are a number of reasons for this rule being on the list. The first is for safety – two heads are better at dealing with a situation than one. Another reason is that there is nothing worse than seeing a fox or a bouncing herd of deer and having no one to share it with. Also it's good to have someone to talk to and laugh with – it makes even the wettest day sunny.

Equipment

You don't need much equipment if you are just going out to collect a few blackberries, but with time you will start to acquire pieces of kit that make your life easier – anything from a favourite wicker basket to a pair of snazzy secateurs. I always make it up as I go along, but there are a few essentials I never leave home without: a basket, a selection of carrier bags, scissors, a pocket knife and a walking-stick. The walking-stick is essential for moving undergrowth or pulling down tall branches. If you don't have one you can easily make one (see page 89) – I usually make a new one every trip. Apart from the equipment I use for collecting, cutting and carrying, there is another item you should take with you and that is a decent guidebook. This should be the first bit of kit you acquire, and one of the best ones around is Food for Free by Richard Mabey. The good thing about such books, apart from the detailed identification of various plants, both edible and poisonous, is that they are pocket-sized. The last thing you want to deal with when trying to identify a certain wild food is large floppy pages, especially when it starts raining or the wind gets up.

Cutting a Walking-stick

A walking-stick will quickly become an essential part of your kit when you go in search of wild food, as well as being a good companion on a country stroll. You will soon find all kinds of uses for it – holding back the foliage of a bush, knocking down hazelnuts, lowering the branches of a tree to get at the ripest fruit. It can be as simple or complicated as you want it to be, allowing you to develop a craft and add some individuality to your creation. A walking-stick that you have hand-crafted yourself makes a wonderful personalized present, and it won't cost you a penny.

The best wood to use is hazel, because it's flexible when green, very abundant, and has many straight, upright branches. The best time to cut your stick is in late autumn, when the tree is dormant and the wood has very little sap in it. The easiest stick to cut is a simple shaft. You can leave the bark on or take it off, or you can cut a pattern into it with a knife. You can cut your stick and use it immediately if you like, but if you want it to last you will need to season the wood and dry it out.

The next kind of stick is the thumb stick, so called because it has a Y-fork at the end for your thumb to fit into, giving a better grip and support. The Y-fork is also excellent for reaching apples or lifting mushrooms off the ground. You need to find a long straight branch that splits in half at one end, with the halves at around a 45° angle to each other. When you cut the stick from the tree, with the straight main shaft and the section where the branch splits into two, make sure the smaller branches are at least six or seven inches in length – you can cut them to the right size later. A good tip before you cut your stick is to pop your thumb into the Y-fork to make sure you get a comfortable fit, as this will reduce the carving you will have to do later.

To make a stick with a curved handle is a little more complicated and will require a lot more work on your part, but the finished product will be even more rewarding and treasured. When cutting your stick, part of the main branch or root must be included as this will form the handle. You want to end up with the straight shaft and a block of wood at the end – this will give you plenty of excess to prevent cracking and possible slip-ups while shaping your handle.

Sometimes you will know exactly the design you want and you may wish to make drawings, and at other times you may just make it up as you go along. If you remove the bark from your stick you can smooth it down with sandpaper, and if you really want your walking-sticks to last it's a good idea to put a coat of preservative on them, such as varnish or beeswax. To stop the base of the stick getting split and damaged you can put a metal cap over the end, but it's not essential.

in the wild

Wild Foods Through the Seasons
Spring

Spring is one of my favourite seasons – it's like the return of a welcome friend, helping you forget the cold and dark of winter and filling you with vigour and excitement for the coming year. Days begin to get longer and the sun starts to warm the ground, life is everywhere and the world seems to be in bloom. It's a busy time on the farm, with new-born lambs appearing and the cattle being turned out from their winter quarters into the fields. It is also a great time for wild food, with a wealth of lush soft shoots, packed with flavour, beginning to poke their green heads through the soil.

Wild garlic or ramsons

You will usually smell this plant before you see it. Wild garlic loves woodlands, especially damp ones, and where the conditions are right you will find it in great abundance. All you have to do is walk through a patch of this plant in the wood and your senses are bombarded as it releases its garlicky odour. It's not advisable to walk through such a wood if you plan an intimate evening with your closest loved one, as a short walk will leave you smelling like a bus full of Frenchmen! However, the French really make the most of this plant, turning it into delicious dishes such as soups and salads, while we Brits pass it by without a second glance. Once you familiarize yourself with it, you will end up trying to use it wherever possible. Wild garlic has dark green leaves and very distinctive white starry flowers on long stems. Every part of the plant is edible, with the leaves being used in sandwiches, salads, soups and stir-fries. They also make great wild garlic butter. The small bulb and the flowers can be used in a similar way, or can be added to olive oil to flavour it for dressings. The flowers added to green salads look and taste fantastic. When you use this plant for cooking you need more than if you use it raw, as it tends to lose its strength with heat.

Stinging nettles

This is such a versatile plant, and has many uses from culinary to medicinal. The German army turned it into fabric during the First World War and used it to produce soldiers' uniforms, when cotton was in short supply. Nettles are not only delicious and nutritious, but they also have many properties beneficial to our health. The Romans used to whip themselves with a bunch of stinging nettles every morning to stimulate good blood circulation. I don't suggest you do this, as you would be in so much pain that the only thing you'd be able to wear would be a toga. However, the plant is in such abundance that you should take advantage of it, and if you have not tasted this garden bully before you are in for a pleasant surprise. Pick only the young fresh growth and avoid the old woody parts of the plant – don't forget to wear gloves! Wash the nettles, put the leaves into a saucepan with a little water and simmer until soft. The leaves can now be used to flavour soups and omelettes, or you can simply eat them as they are with a knob of butter and some salt and freshly ground black pepper.

Fat hen

You will find this dark green succulent plant growing anywhere – in your back garden, on waste ground or beside a country track. Fat hen was once eaten in large quantities but has now been superseded by spinach; however, it contains more iron and protein than spinach and is free to anyone who wants to pick it. Fat hen is easily recognizable, with its branchy growth and its fleshy stems with arrow-shaped leaves. The plant gets its peculiar name from the fact that it was once regularly used to feed chickens, and it is certainly a favourite with my poultry, especially the geese. Whole plants can be used when young; with older plants just take the tender side shoots and cook them like spinach. Great served simply with butter and freshly ground black pepper.

Chickweed

You will find this plant growing in the same areas as fat hen; it can be harvested much later in the year but is at its best in spring, when it's tender enough for the whole plant to be used. Chickweed can be either cooked like spinach or used as an addition to a wild food salad.

Hawthorn

This is a tree that's as common in city gardens and parks as it is in hedgerows and woodlands. Various parts of the tree can be utilized depending on the season. In spring it is the leaf buds and very young leaves that you are after, for their nutty flavour, which is great added to green salads. Be careful when picking, as this tree is well armed with sharp spines.

Dandelion

I was always told as a kid that if you touched the flower of a dandelion it would make you wet the bed, so I spent all my time avoiding the plant in order to keep control of my waterworks. It was only when I grew up that I realized everything my brother had told me was not necessarily true – although dandelion is in fact said to have a diuretic effect if eaten in large quantities. Now that I am better informed I have made proper acquaintance with this plant, which has to be one of the most common species in the UK. The whole plant is edible but it's mostly the young leaves that are eaten, as these are easily added to salads or sandwiches. Alternatively the whole plant, roots included, can be blanched and served as a side vegetable with meat.

Puffball

If you are lucky enough to come across this giant of the fungus world you will know it. I remember one day walking across one of the fields belonging to the agricultural college where my friend Marc Cooper was teaching. With our heads bowed deep in both thought and conversation, we were crossing the paddock when all of a sudden there were these football-sized monster mushrooms at our feet. What a conversation stopper! I picked one of the five fungi and we returned to Marc's flat, where we cut thick steak slices from the huge white puffball, fried them and ate them in a toasted sandwich. You don't want your puffball to be too big, because the flesh becomes less firm. Once picked, wrap it in clingfilm and store it in the fridge. The flesh is great cut into cubes and added to soups or stews, or cut in strips and fried with liver, bacon and black pudding.

Wild Garlic Vinegar

The wood at the farm is full of wild garlic and I've tried using it in thousands of recipes, from the raw leaves in sandwiches to the flowers in stir-fries. This is one of the best, as it lasts for ages and is great for giving a real garlic kick to any salad dressing.

- a large handful of wild garlic leaves and flowers
- 450ml/¾ pint white wine vinegar

Chop the leaves and flowers quite coarsely and then crush them further in a pestle and mortar. Heat half the vinegar to boiling point and pour it on to the garlic. Pound for a moment, then leave to cool. When cool, mix with the rest of the vinegar and pour the lot into a bottle. Leave for 2 weeks, shaking it every 2 or 3 days, then strain and rebottle.

Aromatic Oil with Wild Garlic

Oils can be flavoured with many different herbs, and it's another use for the masses of wild garlic that I have on the farm. It's awesome drizzled over pizza or pasta, or to add a garlic punch when frying steak.

- 450ml/¾ pint olive oil
- 2 branches of fresh rosemary
- 6 sprigs of fresh thyme
- 4 cloves of wild garlic
- 5–6 small chilli peppers
- 6 black peppercorns
- 6 juniper berries

Pour the oil into a glass bottle, stoppered with a cork for preference. Wash the herbs and the garlic well and pat dry. Drop the herbs and spices into the bottle and seal tightly. Keep for at least 2 weeks before using. There is no need to strain.

Pot-roast Pork Fillet with Nettle Stuffing and Cider and Cream Sauce

When I arrived on the farm the place was covered in nettles, over five feet tall in some places, and now that I produce my own pork it just makes sense to put them together – after all, they are both grown on the same farm.

Serves 4

- 2 pork fillets (about 1kg/2lb 3oz in total)
- salt and freshly ground black pepper
- olive oil
- flour
- 300ml/½ pint stock

For the stuffing

- 1 tablespoon chopped onion
- 1 tablespoon olive oil
- 1 teacup of white breadcrumbs
- ½ teacup of chopped nettle tops
- 1 egg yolk

For the sauce

- 15g/½oz butter
- 2 tablespoons finely chopped shallots
- 5 tablespoons cider
- 4 tablespoons single cream

You will need a large, wide, ovenproof pan with a lid for the pork. Preheat the oven to 180°C/350°F/gas mark 4.

Prepare the stuffing: fry the onion in a little oil until soft but not brown. Remove from the heat and add the breadcrumbs, nettle tops and egg yolk. Mix together and season to taste.

Cut the pork fillets lengthways without separating the pieces. Cover the pieces with greaseproof paper or clingfilm and gently bash with a rolling pin to flatten out. Season with salt and freshly ground black pepper, and spread the stuffing over one side of each fillet. Replace the top of the fillet and tie neatly with string.

Heat a little more oil in a large, wide, ovenproof pan. Dust the fillets with flour and brown them all over. Add the stock to the pan, put the lid on and put it into the preheated oven for 45 minutes or until cooked through. Remove the string and leave the pork to rest for 10 minutes in a warm place.

Pour off any excess stock and fat from the pan and return it to the hob. Add the butter and heat until melted. Add the shallots and cook gently for 2 minutes until soft. Add the cider, bring to the boil, and stir for 2 to 3 minutes, scraping up any brown bits from the pan. Stir in the cream and simmer for a minute or two longer. Season to taste.

Slice the fillets on the diagonal and serve with the sauce.

Dandelion and Bacon Salad

These little beauties grow everywhere, even on the scraggiest bit of ground. Mixed with bacon they make a wicked salad, so get out there, start picking and start enjoying!

Serves 2 as a starter

- 115g/4oz dry-cured streaky bacon, diced
- 170g/6oz young dandelion leaves, washed
- sea salt and freshly ground black pepper
- 3 tablespoons olive oil or bacon fat
- 1 tablespoon white wine vinegar

Fry the bacon until crisp and dry. Put the dandelion leaves into a bowl and season with salt and pepper. Turn them gently in the oil or fat and vinegar. Tip in the bacon and mix again gently.

You could make this more substantial by topping it with a soft poached egg or maybe some soft-boiled quails' eggs.

Hawthorn Bud and Bacon Pudding

This may seem a little strange, but give it a go – it's
a recipe that really welcomes the beginning of spring.

Mix the ingredients for the pastry together in a bowl
and make a well in the middle. Add enough water (about
6–7 tablespoons) to make a soft dough. Turn out on to a
floured surface and knead lightly until smooth. Roll out
thinly into an oblong on a floured board.

Cover with the hawthorn buds, pressing them lightly into the
pastry. Spread the bacon over the buds. Damp the edges of
the pastry with water and roll up like a jam roly-poly. Wrap
in greaseproof paper and steam for 1 to 1½ hours. Serve
with a rich gravy.

Serves 4

For the pastry

- 225g/8oz self-raising flour
- 5g/1 teaspoon salt
- 115g/4oz shredded beef suet
- water to mix

For the filling

- 50g/2oz young hawthorn leaf buds
- 3 rashers of dry-cured streaky
  bacon, de-rinded and chopped finely

Hawthorn Flower Liqueur

There's nothing like spring – when the hedgerows are awash with the white blossom of hawthorn it's as though they've been dusted with icing sugar. A great way to capture the wonderful heady scent to be enjoyed throughout the year is to make the flowers into a liqueur.

The blossom should be picked when the scent is strongest and the flowers are dry. Snip the flowers from the stems and pack them loosely into a wide-necked jar. Cover with brandy and add about 15g/ ½oz of sugar to each 300ml/ ½ pint of liquid. Put on the lid and keep in a warm, dark place for a few weeks, turning occasionally to mix in the sugar. Then leave undisturbed for 3 to 4 months. Strain carefully into a clean bottle and cork firmly. It is now ready to drink.

Makes about 300ml/ ½ pint

- may blossom
- brandy
- sugar

Summer

Summer is a glorious season and I love every moment of it, from the bright early mornings to the long balmy evenings. As our summer is often short it's even more precious, and I try and make the most of every second, spending as much time as possible outside. Summer is a time for picnics and long walks – the air fresh and warm and the trees in full leaf, offering welcome shade from the sun. It is also one of the best times to collect wild foods, as there is an abundance of plant growth and many of the bushes begin to break out into fruit. You couldn't ask for more!

Borage

When I moved out of my parents' house I lived in a shared house in Cambridge. I loved it, not only because I was independent for the first time but also because I could start my own small garden there. This was the first time I ever had come across borage, and I hated it because it kept popping up all over my well-kept patch of paradise. However, my view of it rapidly changed once I began to learn more about its properties, especially its aphrodisiac qualities. This medium-sized plant, which is fairly hairy and feels rough to touch, has beautiful tiny bright blue flowers. The young leaves and flowers are great added to salads, and the flowers on their own make an exotic addition to summer cocktails. Although this plant is not strictly a native to Britain, but rather an escapee from gardens, it is commonly found around waste ground.

Crab-apple

I remember playing under and around an old crab-apple tree at school – with its beautiful blossom and twisted branches it was an immediate attraction. We were always told by the caretaker of the school never to eat the fruit, otherwise it would kill us. This fact didn't really concern us, as we were far too busy using the small apples as hand-grenades whenever we played soldiers. It was not until I left school that I learnt that the fruit was in fact not harmful when eaten, although it is bitter and can cause stomach-ache. It's best eaten cooked or made into a jelly. Crab-apples are the mother of all our cultivated apple trees, which have been selectively bred to give us larger, sweeter fruit. Due to this relationship, crab-apple trees will readily cross-pollinate with cultivated apples to form hybrids. True wild crab-apples and their hybrids are often to be found alongside old railway embankments or hedgerows. The fruits are small and rounded and usually yellow in colour, although red fruit is not uncommon.

Red clover

This is a very common plant in the UK, being found in most grasslands, on waste ground and in overgrown gardens. It has connections with luck and happiness, but I have never found a four-leaf clover no matter how hard I've searched. Clover is often sown to produce lush and nutritional grazing for cattle, and it also has the ability to introduce or fix nitrogen into the soil. As a result it is often used as a natural fertilizer, replacing the nutrients that other crops remove. Clover has never really been considered as a human food plant in this country; however, the North American Indians greatly valued it and even had dances to celebrate its arrival. Both the leaves and the flowers of red clover can be eaten in salads, and the really large flowers can be battered and deep-fried.

Elder

The elder has to be one of the most common trees in the country, finding a home in woodlands, hedgerows, gardens and on waste ground. I've even seen it clinging to the side of a railway bridge in mid-air. This modest little tree flowers in early summer, displaying its cream soda blooms and filling the air with a heady scent. It's a smell that conjures up childhood memories of long hot lazy days, and summer would not be summer without it. The flowers are often picked to make elderflower cordial, but they are also fantastic deep-fried in batter (see recipe on page 119) in much the same manner as the Italians cook courgette flowers. After the flowers come clusters of black shiny berries in late summer. I used to pick great bunches of them on the way home from school and scoff the lot until my tongue was red, and it looked as though I had been wearing lipstick. Eating large quantities of elderberries raw will give you stomach-ache, as it did me, but it did not stop me doing the very same thing again next day. The berries add a wonderful sharpness to ice cream and give real interest to a humble apple crumble.

Lime

This tree has nothing to do with the citrus fruit of the same name, as those come from a completely different tree, one that cannot be grown in this country all year round without human help. Limes are often planted along streets to form avenues, but they are also commonplace in most city parks and gardens, as well as in woodland. The flowers of this tree can be made into lime tea, which not only tastes great, especially mixed with a little honey, but also helps digestion and soothes the nervous system. The flowers are out around June and July, and should be collected in full bloom and laid on trays in a shed to dry for a couple of weeks. Lime flowers are not widely collected in this country, mainly because we have forgotten their uses so there is no demand. The story could not be more different across the Channel in France, where people buy great bags of lime flowers from markets where they are displayed in huge piles. It's strange to think that even the most dedicated urbanite in France still knows about wild food, while we will walk past an abundance of free food and be none the wiser.

Horseradish

Horseradish is the ultimate sauce to have with roast beef, and when it's homemade it's truly spectacular (see recipe on page 111). It always amazes me how many people have never come across fresh horseradish root or know what the plant looks like, especially when you consider how common it is. Horseradish is to be found in and around most waste ground, on the edges of hedgerows or roadside verges. It is easily recognized by its large elongated leaves, which begin to twist as they grow upwards. The part of the plant you are interested in is its large tap root, which is well hidden under the ground – however, it isn't as simple as pulling up a carrot! The roots are fairly large, and trying to extract the plant by tugging at the leaves will only result in a handful of greenery or a snapped root. The only way to get at it is by carefully digging up the root with a fork or spade. Once you have your root it should be washed and peeled for immediate use or wrapped in clingfilm and stored in the fridge until needed.

Hawthorn

Tender hawthorn leaves can still be had during early summer but become increasingly scarce and tough as the season rolls on. However, this fantastic tree offers further delights first with its flowers and then with its stunning red berries, known as haws. The flowers can be added to salads or made into an infusion for a hawthorn tea, while the haws can be steeped in cheap brandy to make a strong-flavoured liqueur that can be used as a base for the best wild sangria.

in the wild

103

Jew's ears

To look at this fungus, with its unusual rubbery appearance and sinister dark colour, you would imagine it would be poisonous. However, it is perfectly edible and extremely abundant – you'll find it almost anywhere that you find elderberry trees, as it is the branches of this tree that the fungus grows on. Choose young Jew's ears, as the older ones will be too tough to eat. Remove them from the branch with a knife, discard any dry or hard bits and wash before cooking. They're great added to soups and stews.

Water mint

Water mint, as its name suggests, is found in and around water. We have large clumps of it growing round our wildlife pond at the farm, and it releases its scent whenever you brush up against it. Mint has a million uses, especially in the kitchen: it's wonderful chopped and added to boiled potatoes and rice dishes, and it can be made into mint sauce and served with lamb, bruised and added to cocktails (especially good with vodka), and made into mint tea. Water mint is easy to identify not only from its distinctive smell, which has a peppermint quality to it, but also by the crown of pink flowers growing in fine little bushes at the top of each stem.

Wild strawberry

This plant is the wild ancestor of the cultivated form of strawberry, and is common in many parts of the UK. Despite being smaller they have a much more delicate flavour. The fruits appear from late June to the end of August, and they make a real treat when you come across a patch on a long summer walk.

Wild fennel

Fennel is such a beautiful and elegant herb, with its feathery branches swaying in the breeze. Wild fennel is commonly found around the coast, which is great as it goes so well with fresh fish. The plant has an unmistakable aniseed smell that will often make you aware of it before you actually see it, and these aromatic qualities become stronger when it's dried. All parts of the plant are edible, but you will find the bulb disappointing if you are expecting the large juicy ones that you get in fruit and vegetable shops – wild fennel has a small bulb. Large fennel bulbs are from a cultivated species known as Florence fennel.

Parasol mushroom

I am in no way a mushroom expert, so I have two simple pieces of advice for you to make sure you don't eat poisonous fungi. The first is to stick to what you know, the second is to take someone with you who knows his puffballs from his honey fungus. I have a mad Italian friend called Gennaro who is a real expert on wild food but specializes in mushrooms. I know of several instances when he has come across other mushroom-hunters and relieved them of a number of fungi that were destined for their table but would have resulted in their funeral. The parasol mushroom was one of the very first mushrooms Gennaro ever showed me, and one I now feel comfortable collecting myself. Delicious and easily spotted from July onwards, it grows in pasture, where it pokes its head well above the grass, and woodland. You should really pick the mushrooms before they open up their caps, and one should be enough for each person. The flesh is delicate and is very good cooked with dry-cured bacon and black pudding.

Trout with Rosemary

I think I prefer trout to salmon – I find it sweeter and I like having a whole fish on my plate. Despite usually being cooked with red meat or poultry, rosemary goes really well with trout and permeates the delicate flesh of the fish. Deliciously simple!

Serves 1

- 1 large sprig of fresh rosemary
- 1 whole trout, cleaned
- salt and freshly ground black pepper

Put the sprig of rosemary inside the trout and season with salt and freshly ground black pepper. Wrap the fish in clingfilm, put it on a plate and store it in the fridge for about an hour, or until ready to cook, so that the flavour of the rosemary infuses the fish.

Cook under a hot grill or on a barbecue for 3 to 4 minutes each side, depending on the size of the fish.

Sea Bass with Wild Fennel

When I first arrived at the farm I use to cook all my meals on the open fire. As most of the buildings were derelict, there were lots of bricks and tiles lying around and I soon found that the large old roof tiles made fantastic grills and hotplates, ideal for cooking fish on. Before you use your chosen roof tile, which should be one of those old terracotta types, not the modern slate ones, it needs to be cleaned. It's tempting to run it under a hot tap and give it a scrub, but as the tile will absorb water that will cause it to crack almost as soon as you put it on the fire. The tile will crack eventually, but it will take a lot longer and be far less violent – all you will know about it will be a faint noise that sounds a bit like snapping a stick. The best way to clean your tile is first to use a brush and then to put it on the fire for a few seconds on each side – this allows the flames to sterilize the surface. If you haven't got a tile, a griddle pan on the barbecue will do the job just as well.

Serves 1–2, depending on the size of your fish

You can use most fish for this dish, and prawns work very well too, with fennel being replaced with bunches of fresh coriander. I chose sea bass, as its delicious firm flesh lends itself so well to barbecuing or cooking over an open fire. A 1kg/2lb 3oz fish will easily be enough for two and will make a huge meal for one.

Once your fire has died down to expose its hot embers, put your tile on the fire and allow it to heat up while you prepare the fennel. I have described wild fennel and its habits on page 104, and you can also buy fresh fennel, but you really want the stalks as much as the lovely green foliage, so make sure you get a good bunch. Snap or cut the fennel to size and lay it over the tile, which should be nice and hot by now. The fennel will act like a protective bed, preventing burning, and will also keep the fish moist during cooking. Once your fennel is in place, lay your fish over the top and allow it to cook on each side for around 15 to 20 minutes, depending on the heat of your fire. To speed up the cooking process you can place another tile over the top – this is especially effective if the tiles are slightly bowed so that they encase the fish. When the fish is cooked, the white flesh should come away from the bones with ease. I eat it as it is, with just a squirt of lemon and some crusty bread.

Horseradish Sauce

Homemade horseradish sauce will blow your head off! Don't get me wrong, it's not because it is too hot, although it does have a real kick, but because there are flavours in the real McCoy that a mass-produced jar can never emulate. What's more, it's free and grows wild just about everywhere.

Makes about 300ml/ ½ pint

- 300ml/ ½ pint soured cream
- 1½–2 tablespoons grated horseradish
- sea salt and freshly ground black pepper
- 1–2 teaspoons lemon juice

Pour the soured cream into a bowl and stir until smooth, then stir in the horseradish bit by bit until your sauce has the desired strength. Add seasonings and lemon juice to taste.

Keep refrigerated and use within 2 to 3 days.

Samphire

Cooking samphire is a little bit like cooking asparagus. In fact, the Romans used to call it 'sea asparagus'.

If the plants are large, look out for the woody stems which should be trimmed off. Smaller, younger samphire plants should be fine. Give them a good old wash to get rid of any seaweed, sand or creatures. Bring a large pan of salted water to the boil then add the samphire. Simmer for about 3 minutes then drain and serve drizzled with melted butter and sprinkled with freshly ground black pepper.

Spiced Crab-apples

At school we used to use these miniature apples as substitute hand-grenades in our war games during playtime. As well as being excellent pretend explosives, they are delicious preserved in their own syrup.

- 2.7 kg/6lb trimmed crab-apples
- 3 strips of lemon rind
- 450g/1lb sugar
- 450ml/¾ pint red wine vinegar
- 1 cinnamon stick
- 2 whole cloves
- 3 peppercorns

Simmer the crab-apples and the lemon rind in a preserving pan with 900ml/1½ pints of water until just tender. Remove the pan from the heat and strain the apples, reserving the liquid. Put the sugar and the vinegar into the pan and add 900ml/1½ pints of the liquid saved from the fruit.

Tie the spices in a piece of muslin and add to the liquid. Stir over a gentle heat until all the sugar has dissolved, then bring up to the boil and boil for 1 minute. Return the crab-apples to the pan and simmer gently for 30 to 40 minutes, until the syrup has reduced and is coating the fruit. Remove the muslin bag after 30 minutes.

Pack the fruit into small sterilized jars and pour over the syrup. Cover with airtight and vinegar-proof tops.

Wild Strawberry Syllabub

Wild strawberries are such a treat when you find them – smaller than their cultivated cousins but so flavoursome and sweet. Try not to eat them all as you collect them!

This light, fluffy dessert is a twist on plain old strawberries and cream.

With a fork, crush the strawberries in a measuring jug and add enough wine to reach the 200ml/⅓ pint mark. Add the sugar and stir until it has dissolved. In a bowl, whip the cream until it stands in stiff peaks. Fold in the strawberry mixture until well mixed. Divide between four glasses and chill in the fridge for at least 4 hours. Some of the wine will separate out at the bottom of the glass.

Serves 4

- 170g/6oz ripe wild strawberries
- medium or sweet white wine
- 15g/½oz caster sugar
- 300ml/½ pint double cream

Elderflower Fritters

In early summer the air is filled with the intoxicating cream soda scent of these beautiful white flowers. For years people have been picking them and turning them into cordials and wine – even champagne-style. One of the best ways to enjoy their flavour is to deep-fry them in a light batter, a bit like the Italians do with courgette flowers.

Serves 4

• 12 elderflower heads (keep short stalks on for dipping)
• oil for deep-frying • icing or caster sugar for dusting

For the batter:
• 4 tablespoons plain flour • pinch of salt • 1 egg • 340ml/12fl oz water

To make the batter, sift the flour into a bowl with the salt. Make a well and break the egg into the middle. Mix, then add the water bit by bit to make a smooth batter. Dip each flower head into the batter, holding it by the stalk, shaking off any excess. Drop the flower heads into a large pan of oil heated to 180°C/360°F. Fry in small batches and drain on kitchen paper, keeping them warm while frying the rest.

Sprinkle with sugar and serve immediately. Lovely with strawberries.

Autumn

Once the corn has been harvested and the nights start to have a chill about them, you begin to sense the approach of autumn. It has to be one of the most dramatic, romantic and reflective of all the seasons, with the change in the trees as the leaves turn from green to red and golden yellow. I love watching this transformation being played out in our woodland – slowly but surely the interior of the wood is exposed and a secret world, once hidden by a thick canopy of green, is exposed. It is also a bumper time to collect wild food, and a chance to stockpile ready for the long cold winter ahead.

Blackberry

Blackberries are a real contrast between pain and pleasure – pleasure from the succulent flavour of the fruit, and pain from the scratches of the thorns as you try to get at the berries. The first summer we had on the farm was very hot and seemed to go on for ever, so much so that come autumn there was a bumper crop of blackberries, the sweetest I'd ever tasted. Blackberry bushes, or brambles as they are commonly known, grow anywhere and everywhere they can; they have an extremely invasive nature and will soon take over a garden if not kept in check.

Poppies

This is a plant that has a special place in our nation's heart. It is associated with the remembrance of fallen soldiers, as its blood-red flowers were found growing on old battlefields. The reason why poppies grew on old battle sites such as the Somme is because the seeds germinate freely in areas where the ground has recently been disturbed, so all the activity of bombs and artillery during a battle would create ideal conditions for them. Such conditions are also created when a field is ploughed by a tractor – the result is a huge red carpet around the edges of the crop, adding a real splash of colour to the countryside. You can't eat the plant itself, but once it has dropped its petals the dry seedheads can be collected and the small seeds can be sprinkled over bread dough before it is baked.

Fennel seeds

After its display of yellow flowers, fennel seeds can be collected in October. You should collect the seeds before they dry out completely – they can be used straight away or dried further and stored. I use fennel seeds when I'm cooking pork, smashing them up with a little sea salt, olive oil and garlic and rubbing the mixture all over the skin before roasting.

Hazelnuts

One of the first jobs I had to do when I arrived on the farm was to clear an area of ground for two mobile homes to be sited, as the farmhouse was in no fit state to be inhabited. The area I chose was an impenetrably thick tangle of trees and bushes. After a day or so of hacking and sawing I discovered that the plot was in fact a derelict orchard, and growing right at the back was a distinguished old hazel tree. What a find – that autumn the old hazel had produced a crop of nuts that kept the six of us munching for weeks. I wait in anticipation every year for the young green nuts to appear and then fatten ready for picking, but I have to be quick if I'm to beat the local squirrels, who will also be waiting to exploit such a rich harvest. The nuts are not only great eaten fresh but can also be roasted, bashed up and mixed with stuffing, or chopped and added to yoghurt with a drizzle of runny honey. The hazel is found growing in most hedgerows and woodlands, and the branches make the best walking-sticks.

Sweet chestnut

The chestnut is one of my favourite wild foods – it brings back wonderful memories of my childhood, when my mum would take me as a special treat to Harrods to see the lights and I would always get a bag of hot chestnuts. I remember walking along the street looking skyward at the department store's illuminations while at the same time trying to peel the piping hot and charred outer shell, desperate to get at the delicious nut inside. At the farm we have masses of sweet chestnut trees – they make up the majority of our woodland, and the nuts are eagerly sought by the foraging pigs, as well as myself. However, getting at the fallen nuts is a tricky and often painful business, as most are still in their prickly husks, surrounded by hundreds of needle-like spines. The best trick I've found is to roll the chestnuts round on the floor with the sole of my boot, applying enough pressure to force the nuts out. They can be pickled or roasted and either eaten as they are or added to stuffing. They can be stored in buckets of sand, which not only helps prevent them shrivelling but also stops any hungry mouse raiding your store. One note of caution: if you intend to roast chestnuts on an open fire you must slit the brown shell with a knife, otherwise they will explode and shower you in fragments of hot nut and shell.

Field mushroom

This is a fairly common mushroom found in lush grasslands and pasture, and can often be confused with other species that may cause you stomach-ache. Field mushrooms should be white in colour, although as they get older they often develop a brown centre on top. The gill-like structure of the mushroom underneath should be pink when young, but with age it becomes brown and then black. There should never be any yellow in the flesh, or any bright yellow colouring at the base of the stalk when you cut it with a knife, as this indicates that it is not a field mushroom and should be discarded.

Beef steak fungus

This is a wonderful-looking fungus that is very characteristic of oak woodland and is found growing on the sides of old oaks or sweet chestnuts. The brackets (the term for the part of the fungus that is visible growing on the outside of the tree) appear on the bark of the tree, often around the base, though I have also seen them growing fairly high up, from late summer all the way through autumn. Over time the fungus dies and comes crashing down, and as a result dead and rotting beef steak fungus can often be found on the woodland floor – however, this is not for eating. You really want to cut beef steak fungus from the tree when it is young and not rubbery; use a sharp knife, but be careful not to damage the tree. The fungus gets its name from the fact that when you cut it open the flesh looks very similar to well-grained beef, although you will be disappointed if you are expecting the taste to be the same as beef – it has a bitter quality due to its acidity. Beef steak fungus is best sliced and fried with lots of garlic – add a splash of cream to the pan at the end of cooking and serve on toast.

Juniper

The juniper is a small evergreen tree that produces small blue berries. These are the main flavouring of one of my favourite drinks, and that's gin. The berries are on the trees in September and October – they have a bittersweet quality and are great added to bacon and ham cures, or crushed and cooked with game.

Wild rose

After flowering, the dog rose produces shiny bright red rosehips that contain twenty times more vitamin C than an orange. The fruit is best picked after the first frosts, when the hips will have been softened. Rosehips make fantastic jellies – a great accompaniment to game such as pheasant.

in the wild

123

Wild Mushrooms on Toast

Although they can be cooked in lots of ways and can enrich many dishes, I like to cook freshly picked wild mushrooms very simply. There is no need to add other flavours or ingredients – the earthy richness is a taste to savour unsullied. One of my favourite ways to enjoy them is fried in butter and eaten on hot buttered toast – a treat that cannot be beaten!

Whether you have bought your mushrooms or have picked them yourself, you need to give them a clean. Check them to make sure they are not damaged, mouldy or infested with any unwanted creatures, then use a damp cloth or a soft brush to wipe away any dirt, soil or other debris. Cut away any bits that look dodgy. Do not wash them or they will go soggy.

Melt a good knob of butter in a frying pan. When it is bubbling, add the mushrooms and stir. Fry for about 5 to 6 minutes until they are soft and the juices start to run. Season to taste with salt and pepper.

Pile on to hot buttered toast and tuck in!

Serves 2

- 340g/12oz fresh mixed wild mushrooms
- 30g/1oz butter, plus a bit more for buttering the toast
- salt and freshly ground black pepper
- 4 slices of bread (slices from a good old-fashioned uncut white loaf do it for me!)

Candied Chestnuts

Autumn on the farm means chestnuts! We have around thirty acres of woodland, predominantly made up of sweet chestnut, but we have to work fast if the pigs aren't to eat the lot. You can preserve these beautiful dark brown nuts by burying them in dry sand, but I love to candy them. The process does take a few days, but the results are well worth it.

- 600g/1lb 5oz fresh, peeled chestnuts
- 450g/1lb granulated sugar

Put the chestnuts into a large saucepan, cover them with cold water and bring to the boil. Reduce the heat to a simmer and cook for about 20 minutes, until tender. Do not overcook, otherwise they will break up during candying. Drain them, reserving about 150ml/¼ pint of the cooking water.

Return the cooking water to the pan and add the sugar. Stir over a gentle heat until all the sugar has dissolved. Add the chestnuts, bring to the boil, and remove from the heat. Cover the pan and leave in a warm place for 24 hours.

On the second day, repeat the process of bringing the pan to the boil. Remove from the heat, cover the pan and leave for another 24 hours.

On day three, repeat the boiling process but then remove the chestnuts from the pan with a slotted spoon. Place them on a wire rack over a tray and leave them to dry in a warm place for a couple of days. They are ready when they are no longer sticky.

The candied chestnuts should be stored in cardboard or wooden boxes, interleaved with waxed paper or non-stick parchment – airtight containers may make them go mouldy.

Sloe Gin

I was introduced to sloe gin when I was working at a wildlife park. There was a lovely lady called Violet who used to take the entrance money at the gate, and each week she would bring me something she had made – anything from jam to bread rolls. One week she brought a bottle without any label, filled with a deep red liquid. I never asked the alcohol content, but when I had lost the power of speech after a few glasses I guessed it was pretty strong. You can drink sloe gin as it is, but I find it a little sweet so I use it as a mixer to make a mean sloe gin and tonic with loads of ice.

Choose ripe sloes and wash, dry and prick them. Fill the bottles halfway up with the fruit and sugar and top up with the gin. Cork well and store in a moderately warm place for 3 months, shaking occasionally. After 3 months minimum (the best sloe gin is said to be kept for a year), strain the gin through muslin into a clean bottle.

Makes 2 bottles

- 450g/1lb sloes
- 170g/6oz sugar
- 1 bottle of gin
- 2 empty bottles

Preserved Elderberries

After its beautiful flowers, the elder tree rewards us with clusters of shiny, juicy black berries. My mum always told me they were poisonous and that I was never to touch them, but I refused to believe her and I used to eat great bunches on the way home from school. However, they did give me belly-ache.

Wash the berries under cold running water to remove any grime or creepy-crawlies. Shake off excess water and strip the berries from the stems. Layer the berries and the sugar together to fill the jar(s). Cover with foil and put in a warm oven, or stand the jars in a pan of hot water until the juice begins to run. Seal the jars while still hot. Cool and store in a cold place until required. The fruit can be used with apples, in pies or poured over ice cream.

Makes 1 large or 2 small jars

• 900g/2lb elderberries
• 115g/4oz sugar
• sterilized jar or jars

Blackberry Junket

Bramble is a plant that invades most gardens, especially urban ones, and I have spent hours cutting it back, being torn to ribbons and cursing as I go. However, all is forgiven once this invader produces big fat sweet berries ripe for the picking. Junket is traditionally made with milk and rennet, but this method produces a lovely fruity result.

Juice the berries in a juicer or by pressing through muslin. Allow the juice to stand in a warm room for several hours undisturbed, without stirring or adding anything. It will set to the consistency of a light junket and is great with cream and biscuits.

Winter

With the run-up to Christmas, winter really gives you the feeling of closure on another year. It's a time for rest and reflection, a time to meet up with friends and family for lavish feasts and good times. It's also a time when the countryside begins to slow down, as the nights draw in and the cold weather really takes a hold. The cold weather not only brings numb fingers and red noses but also serves to kill many insect pests and harmful fungi that would otherwise remain unchecked. There are very few wild foods around at this time of year, as most plants have shut up shop for winter and most of the nuts, seeds and berries have dropped or been eaten. Trees begin to go into a state of dormancy, and most have become completely bare, exposing their skeleton of branches. It's a time to conserve resources and rely on stored foods that have been harvested during the bountiful periods – pickles, chutneys, jams and jellies are brought out to bring back memories of summer. Other stored treasures such as chestnuts and dried mushrooms, herbs and seeds are called on to provide much-needed protein and flavouring during the bleak winter months. Although wild greens may be at a premium during winter, it is a bumper time for wild meats because the coming of winter heralds the beginning of the shooting season.

Wild meat or game

Whether you are in favour of hunting and shooting or against, it is important for the countryside that certain animals are culled. If you don't shoot, it doesn't mean you cannot get your hands on some game, as it is readily available during the shooting season from farm shops, farmers' markets, local butchers and game dealers. I know this isn't directly collecting it yourself, but it is still classed as wild food. If you want to find out more about shooting, get in touch with the Game Conservancy Trust and the British Association for Shooting and Conservation.

Rabbit

Forty or fifty years ago rabbit was a common dish in every house, as much as any other kind of meat. During the Second World War my grandfather was serving with the Royal Air Force, guarding our airfields and coastline from night bombing raids by enemy aircraft. During the day, apart from sleeping, he and his pals use to hunt rabbits, which they sent home, and my nan used to receive a rabbit in the post every couple of weeks. However,

it was not long before rabbits became a real agricultural pest – each doe can give birth to twenty youngsters a year, and each rabbit can start breeding when it's only four months old. Measures were therefore taken to cull the population and the meat fell out of favour. Rabbit is a great favourite of mine, and when I was a student it made up a major part of my weekly menu. Life at university meant that money was always tight, and buying a rabbit was one way I could afford meat from an animal that had led a truly healthy and free-range existence, rather than a cheap chicken that had not. Rabbit is truly delicious, and you get a lot of meat for your money – one large rabbit will just about feed a family of four if made into a stew.

Hare

At first glance hares look like the gangly teenager of the rabbit family – you almost expect them to have bad acne and braces. On closer inspection they are a different animal altogether, much bigger and sleeker, and if disturbed they can shoot off like a rocket, reaching speeds of up to 35mph. Hares, unlike rabbits, live out in the open, completely exposed to weather and predators and relying on speed as their defence. At one time they were extremely rare, due to over-use of pesticides, but in some places – here in Suffolk, for example – they are fairly common now. You can buy hares from game dealers, farmers' markets and some butchers. A friend of mine called Les who runs Furness Fish down at Borough Market always has a good selection of hares, including not only brown hare but also mountain hare, which has a pure white coat in winter. You get a lot more meat on a hare than you do on a rabbit, but the flavour is very similar and it can be treated in the same way. I like to marinate mine in red wine or beef stock for a few days, then slowly pot-roast it and serve it with mashed root vegetables.

Squirrel

Not many people would entertain the thought of eating squirrel, which I find quite odd because it's a wild meat that's regularly eaten in the southern states of the USA. Squirrels can be shot with a .22 air rifle if you have the permission of the landowner, but only grey squirrels, which are an alien species introduced from North America, should be considered as quarry and not the native red, which is endangered. If you don't shoot you will not be able to get your hands on a squirrel as easily as a rabbit or hare, but if you know the right people – gamekeepers, for example – it is relatively easy. Squirrel should be treated in much the same way as rabbit, although the flavour is more perfumed and you will need one per person. I always include a jointed squirrel with mussels, crayfish and plenty of bourbon for a really authentic gumbo.

Deer

In the UK we have six species of deer. Three of them, the red, the fallow and the roe deer, are native, while the Sika (which is similar to the red deer and will interbreed producing fertile hybrids), the muntjac and the Chinese water deer have all been introduced from Asia. After mad cow disease, many people made the change from beef to venison and it is still popular, even to the extent of being stocked in the occasional supermarket. It is a meat that is very low in fat and rich in flavour, and it should be well hung in its fur. Most local butchers will sell venison cut into roasting joints and steaks, as will farm shops and game suppliers at farmers' markets. Most of the venison offered for sale will be farmed, but much is still taken from wild stock, usually one of our native species. Occasionally the odd muntjac will appear, which I find, contrary to other people's opinion, amazing eating. If you have not tried venison, give it a go – you will find it excellent value!

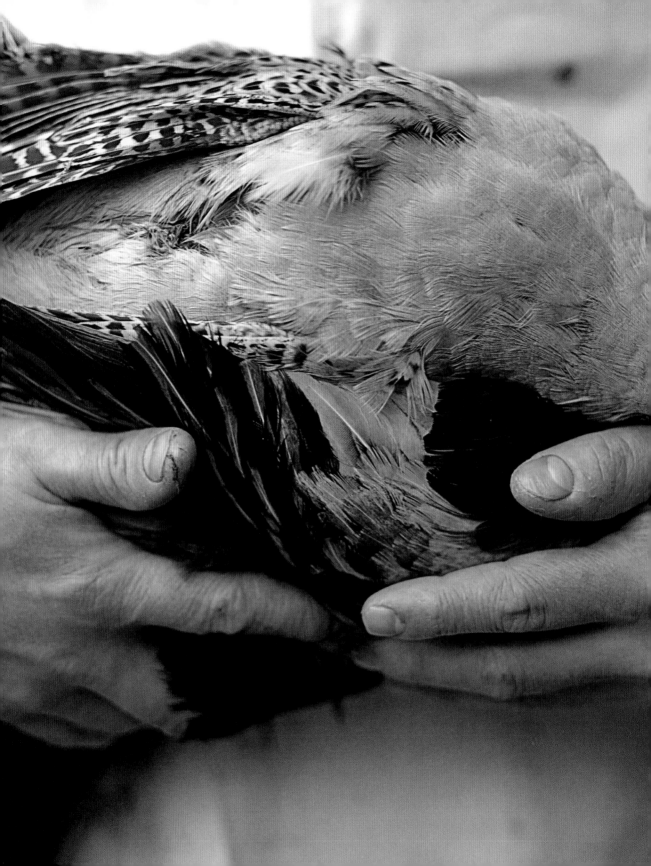

Pheasant

This is a dazzling bird that is not fully appreciated either for the beauty of the male's plumage or for the taste of the meat. During the shooting season the market is awash with pheasants, as organized shoots harvest the birds that the gamekeeper has reared earlier. This is real free-range farming, as once released into the wood the young pheasants are free to roam wherever they wish. The birds that are not taken that season go on to the next season to breed and become part of the wild stock. I don't agree with shooting birds if they are not going to be eaten, as I feel it's a shameful waste in a world where food is a precious commodity. However, shooting, strange as it may sound when it's about the taking of life, has a part to play in conservation. Many woodlands exist in our countryside, especially in arable areas, purely for the rearing and shooting of pheasants, which provides the farmer with a little extra cash as well as the social aspect of getting together with friends. Without the value that comes from rearing these game birds the woodland would have very little use to the farmer, who as a businessman would be better off ploughing it over and planting crops. However, using the remaining woods for shooting ensures their survival, which is crucial for our wildlife – especially when you consider that a third of the world's bluebell population resides in them! If it weren't for the farmers rearing game, who else would preserve the majority of the private woodland in this country?

Although the pheasant is such a characteristic symbol of the British countryside, it is in fact an alien species – it originates in China and belongs to a large family of birds that also includes the stately pea fowl. Pheasants benefit from a week's hanging before cooking, as this helps to tenderize the meat. Otherwise the flesh will be tough, as the bird will have had regular exercise and used its muscles to the full. Pheasant season starts on 1 October and ends on 1 February – during this time the birds are in plentiful supply and are usually sold as pairs or a brace. Many people like to cook their birds in a very rich red wine sauce, which is very traditional and sumptuous; however, I like to lighten the flavour by using lemon and orange zest, with plenty of fresh rosemary and a dash of white wine.

Partridge

We have two species of partridge in the UK: the English or grey, and the French or red-legged. The grey partridge is said to have sweeter meat than its foreign cousin, which was brought to the UK from France by Charles II. However, I have found little to choose between the two species and I prefer to buy the French partridge because the English one has declined in numbers over recent years. Both birds are available between 1 September and 1 February and make excellent eating pot-roasted with figs. You really need to hang your birds for 4 to 5 days before cooking, and one bird per person will be more than ample.

in the wild

Wood pigeon

Wood pigeon numbers are booming, due mainly to all the free food provided by arable farmers – well, this is how the pigeons would see it, though I very much doubt the farmer would take this view. Pigeon is underrated in the UK and is not commonly eaten nowadays, as most people associate pigeons with the moth-eaten birds in Trafalgar Square rather than the plump and richly flavoured wood pigeon. They are staggeringly cheap and are easily available from most farmers' markets a nd good butchers. I wait in a quiet area in the wood where I know the birds will return, and take a couple with my air rifle; however, shooting a bird in flight will require the use of a shotgun, as an air rifle will not be up to the job. If you are averse to shooting or don't have the opportunity, you can buy pigeon complete, or oven-ready, and sometimes you can just buy the breast meat, which is fantastic flashed in a hot pan with a little garlic and butter. Young birds can be roasted, while older individuals will require slow cooking to prevent the meat being too tough.

Duck

Wild duck is not the same as duck that has been farmed – it has a stronger flavour, will be tougher, and the meat is darker and may vary in its eating quality due to the conditions on the water where the bird has spent most of its time feeding. Many species of duck feed around coastlines and estuaries, and such ducks will reflect this in their meat. The species that are commonly available if you don't shoot are mallard, teal and widgeon, and of these three it is the much larger mallard that you are more likely to come across. The mallard is the founding father of most of the domestic ducks that are farmed or kept in private gardens or public parks. As a result it will interbreed with most domestic ducks whenever the chance arises, and when wild females are at a premium rogue males will seek out any opportunity. I have seen wild males fly into my farm, eat my duck food, strut their stuff, act flash, then leave, much to my horror and the horror of my male ducks, accompanied by one of my domestic females. For this reason it is getting harder and harder, apart from the remote areas, to find a mallard that has not got some domestic blood running through its veins. The season for wild mallard is between 1 September and 31 January and you can get them from all good butchers, game dealers and farmers' markets. Your wild bird should ideally hang for 3 days before cooking.

Duck with Figs

Despite being a pig farmer, I have to say duck is one of my favourite meats, full of flavour, with delicious fat and wonderful crispy skin. I have a few breeds of duck on the farm, but for me the best for eating has to be the Muscovy, also known as the Barbary duck.

Serves 4

- 1.8kg/4lb duck with giblets
- salt and freshly ground black pepper
- 1 clove of garlic, sliced
- 2 bay leaves
- 1 orange, quartered
- 1 tablespoon olive oil
- 450ml/¾ pint dry white wine
- 225g/8oz fresh figs, quartered

For the stock

- the duck giblets
- ½ a medium onion, sliced
- 2 carrots, halved
- 2 cloves of garlic, crushed
- ½ teaspoon dried marjoram
- ½ teaspoon dried thyme
- ½ teaspoon salt
- 6 black peppercorns

To make the stock put all the ingredients into a saucepan with 450ml/¾ pint of water and bring to the boil. Skim and reduce to a simmer. Cover and simmer for 45 minutes, skimming occasionally.

Preheat the oven to 170°C /325°F/gas mark 3. Season the cavity of the duck with salt and pepper and put the garlic, bay leaves and orange inside. Truss the legs and prick the skin all over with a fork.

In a casserole, heat up the olive oil and brown the duck all over. Pour off the excess fat. Combine the duck stock and the wine in a saucepan and bring to the boil. Pour over the duck in the casserole dish. Cover and cook in the oven for 1½ to 2 hours, until the juices run clear when the inside of the leg is pierced with a skewer.

Remove the duck to a plate, take off the string and keep warm.

Skim the fat off the juices remaining in the casserole. Add the figs and bring back to the boil. Once the figs are heated through and the sauce has thickened, pour it all over the duck and serve immediately.

Pheasant with Red Wine and Raisins

Pheasants have great flavour, lead a truly free-range life eating wild foods, and are ridiculously cheap! For the price of two skinless chicken breasts from factory-farmed birds that have led a miserable life, you can buy two whole healthy pheasants that will actually taste of something . . . it's a mad world! There are endless ways of cooking these birds, from roasting to curries, but here is one of my favourites.

Serves 2 generously

- 2 hen pheasants
- 1 tablespoon flour
- salt and freshly ground black pepper
- 15g/½oz butter
- 1 tablespoon vegetable oil
- 300ml/½ pint chicken stock

For the marinade

- 300ml/½ pint red wine
- 3 tablespoons red wine vinegar
- 115g/4oz seedless raisins
- 170g/6oz no-soak dried apricots, halved
- 5ml/1 teaspoon ground ginger
- 5ml/1 teaspoon ground cinnamon
- 1cm/½ inch piece of fresh ginger, peeled and grated
- 4 cloves
- 4 juniper berries, lightly crushed

Combine the marinade ingredients in a bowl. Wash the cavity of the pheasants with water, then put them into a dish and pour in the marinade, spooning it over to ensure that the birds are well covered. Cover and leave to marinate for 3 to 4 hours or overnight, turning occasionally.

Preheat the oven to 180°C/350°F/gas mark 4. Remove the pheasants from the marinade, keeping it for later, and pat the birds dry with kitchen paper. Coat in flour seasoned with salt and freshly ground black pepper.

In a large casserole, heat the butter and oil and brown the pheasants all over. Remove and drain on kitchen paper, then pour off any excess fat remaining in the casserole. Stir in the chicken stock and the reserved marinade, and bring to the boil. Return the pheasants to the pot, cover and cook in the preheated oven for about 1½ hours, or until tender.

Remove the pheasants from the casserole and keep warm. Boil the remaining liquid until thickened and reduced. Carve the pheasants and serve with the sauce.

'Kentucky Fried' Rabbit

Sorry about the name! If you have never eaten rabbit before, this is a brilliant recipe to get you started. It is a great way of cooking wild rabbit, which can be a bit tough – if you are using farmed rabbit it will need less boiling.

Bring a large pan of water to the boil. Add the rabbit pieces and simmer until tender – about 5 to 8 minutes. Drain and set aside.

Mix the breadcrumbs, Parmesan, salt and freshly ground black pepper together in a shallow bowl. Put the beaten egg and the flour into separate shallow bowls too.

When cool, dip each rabbit piece first in the flour, then in the egg and finally in the breadcrumb mixture, ensuring they are evenly coated. Heat a couple of tablespoons of sunflower oil and a knob of butter in a large frying pan and fry the rabbit pieces over a gentle heat, turning occasionally, until crisp and golden (about 8 minutes).

Serve with a green salad and lemon wedges.

Serves 2

- 1 rabbit, jointed into small pieces
- 85g/3oz breadcrumbs
- 85g/3oz Parmesan cheese, finely grated
- salt and freshly ground black pepper
- 2 eggs, beaten
- 3 tablespoons plain flour
- butter and sunflower oil for frying

Braised Pigeon

When most people think of pigeon they think of those tatty little birds that mass in city centres and pick through the rubbish on the streets, but the pigeon we eat is a completely different creature. The wild wood pigeon is a much larger, plump-breasted bird that spends its days flying across open countryside from one wooded patch to another in search of wild foods – and farmers' crops! When cooked properly the meat is tender, sweet and full of flavour, and what's more it's incredible value, one of nature's wonder foods! This is a great way to cook pigeon – it keeps all its natural flavours but also infuses them with beautiful fresh herbs.

Serves 4

- 4 slices of dry-cured streaky bacon
- 45g/1½oz butter
- 115g/4oz button mushrooms
- 4 young pigeons
- 1 tablespoon flour
- salt and freshly ground black pepper
- 1 medium onion, chopped
- 185ml/6½fl oz of white wine
- fresh lemon thyme, parsley, marjoram
- a pinch of ground nutmeg
- a pinch of ground allspice
- rind of ½ a lemon, plus a squeeze of juice

Preheat the oven to 180°C/350°F/gas mark 4.

In a heavy casserole, fry the bacon in 30g/1oz of butter for a couple of minutes. Add the mushrooms and cook for a few more minutes until lightly browned. Dust the pigeons with seasoned flour and brown in the remaining butter until sealed on all sides. Remove the pigeons, bacon and mushrooms from the pan and set aside for a moment.

Add the onion to the pan and fry until tender but not brown. Return the mushrooms and bacon to the pan, sit the pigeons on top, and pour over the white wine. Add the herbs, spices, lemon rind and juice and season with salt and freshly ground black pepper. Bring to a simmer, cover the casserole and braise for about 1 hour or until tender.

The Great Outdoors

For me, being in the great outdoors is every bit as natural and as comforting as sitting on the sofa with a nice cup of tea. I feel at home and completely safe wandering through nature's wildernesses, so much so that I'd feel more secure walking through a woodland in the dead of night than through one of our city centres. I suppose we only fear the unknown or unfamiliar, but once we begin to explore and increase our understanding, our fears diminish.

There is something wonderful, even magical, about being amidst nature – you get a sense of belonging and feel part of the landscape and environment. I believe everyone has the ability to feel such a connection with the natural world, however urbanized they may be. For example, take my great friend Simon Willis: at first sight he appears to be the most unlikely outdoor person, with his mobile phone in one hand and a skinny-mocha-choca-Americana (or whatever the bloody name is for those overpriced coffees) in the other. When he visited the farm recently I took him exploring through my wood, and Simon spent the first hour stumbling over logs, frantically wiping spider's webs from his hair and worrying about being attacked by wild creatures. However, after a couple of hours he began to relax and get the feel of his surroundings. You could literally see his shoulders slowly drop as the stress of urban life ebbed away, to be replaced by natural sensations that soothed and exhilarated. At first he was a real fish out of water, but within a few hours he looked as though a walk in the wood was just as much a part of his normal routine as his daily commute into London.

As a child the great outdoors was simply an extended playground where my imagination could run wild – one minute I was leading an army of knights into battle, the next I was on safari in deepest Africa. The greatest adventures were always those occasions when a group of us would camp

out for the night. We would fill our backpacks with sleeping-bags, bottles of squash, sausages, eggs, frying pans and anything else that our mums wouldn't miss, then we would all set off. I remember arriving at our chosen site feeling as though we had crossed continents, climbed mountains to reach this foreign land, despite only being in a field in the next village! The most important part of these childhood adventures, and of the numerous camping trips I've been on since, has always been cooking the food over the open campfire. It's an experience you never forget, and it is this feeling that inspired me to write this chapter. I want everyone to experience and enjoy cooking as nature intended, out in the open, whether on a beach over a campfire, or in your backyard on a simple barbecue. Wherever it is, all that matters is that you have good food, great company and the open sky above.

The Campfire

The day man discovered fire was a point in history that changed our destiny as a species for ever. Before that, life must have been very different for mankind, especially when night fell. For early humans it must have been an unnerving experience trying to sleep out in the open, defenceless, with no idea what was watching and waiting for them to close their eyes and drift off. Fire gave security; it was a light during the hours of darkness, burning brightly and keeping predators such as wolves, bears and lions at bay while they slept safely. Fire also offered warmth, allowing mankind to venture further into colder climates to explore new hunting-grounds and territories which would otherwise have been impossible. Fire also had an effect on us socially: man was able to sit around the fire and relax, talk, sing, discuss ideas and tell stories that ultimately led to the development of culture. There is something awe-inspiring about sitting round an open fire watching the flames rising up into the night sky as our ancestors did before us – it's one of those rare occasions where we can connect with our ancient past. Early man soon discovered that by putting various plants and animal parts on the fire he could make them more palatable or even turn the inedible edible. This was the start of cooking, and from that point the rest is history, all the way up to the dizzy heights of the celebrity chefs.

I love getting back to cooking at grass-roots level, and my outdoor cooking experience doesn't start with the ingredients, or even the pots and pans, but rather with the building of the fire and selecting the right fuel for the job. There is a certain skill to laying a fire, and how you construct it depends on what you want to achieve. If it's a simple bonfire you just need to stack everything up willy-nilly like a wigwam. However, if you want to cook over the fire or boil water you will need to have control over it, rather than building a massive blaze that you can't get near.

Building a fire

Fire can be a very destructive force, as I found out to my horror during my first year at the farm when a bonfire got out of control and with the help of the wind quickly spread across one of my fields. Man has the power to create fire, and with great power comes great responsibility. Before building any fire, select a suitable site. If you are not building the fire on your own property, you must first get permission from whoever owns the land or campsite before you even consider striking a match. Many public campsites have designated areas for lighting campfires, or barbecue facilities, and it is well worth a little research before setting off on a trip. Site selection is important with respect to protecting the surrounding flora as well as your own safety. Here are some points for you to consider before you get going, but don't assume this is a comprehensive list – there may be points you want to add that have relevance to your particular conditions.

1. Never site a fire directly under the branches of a tree. The heat generated from a fire set too close to a tree can cause a lot of damage, not only to the tree trunk and the branches above but also to all the wildlife that has taken refuge amongst its foliage, such as nesting birds.

2. Never light a fire too near standing crops. If you light a fire too close to a wheat field you run a real risk of causing thousands of pounds' worth of damage and getting yourself into serious trouble. It's common sense really – areas such as crops, tall grass, stubble fields should all be avoided, especially in dry weather!

3. Make sure you are close to a water source, such as a garden hose, tap or river – this will allow you to put out a fire fast as well as providing a means of washing up. If you are going to start a fire you should always have a way of putting it out. I always have a spade and bucket handy. You can fill the bucket with soil if water is unavailable, and it can be used at any time to smother the flames. Once I've finished with the fire I dig over it to put it out, patting it gently every now and then to starve it of oxygen.

4. Don't site your fire too close to a dwelling. The obvious reason for this is so that you don't set your house alight. There is also nothing worse than spreading smoke across someone's garden, especially if they have their windows open or their washing out.

5. Always clear combustible material from your chosen fire site and around its immediate area. This is vital, as environments like the floor of a woodland clearing or old grassland are covered with dead dry leaves that form a deep litter. The danger here is that your fire could spread very easily through this leaf litter without you even realizing, smouldering out of sight beneath the dead plant material only to reappear a little distance away.

6. Dig out your site. If you want to be extra cautious you can always dig a small pit in the ground. Usually I get my spade and dig a square patch out of the ground where I'm going to light my fire, making it slightly bigger than the actual fire will be. I lift out the whole slab of earth, complete with its covering vegetation, and place it carefully to one side. When my fire's finished I neatly replace the square patch of earth intact, with its green grass on top, so that you would never know there had been a fire at all!

Selecting your fuel

All types of wood are different – it depends on what tree species it has been collected from. Some are dense and burn slowly, for example hardwoods such as oak, while others contain resins and spit and crackle and will burn quickly, such as the softwoods. For cooking you need a slow-burning wood, to provide a good heat over a length of time. However, for boiling water you can use lighter timber that will burn fast and brightly, such as pine – this will give you the punch of power needed to boil a kettle.

Slow-burning hardwoods: ash, beech, birch, sweet chestnut and oak.

Fast-burning softwoods: pine, alder, hawthorn and poplar.

Collecting firewood

There are many ways of getting hold of wood for your fire, but one of the easiest is to collect it yourself. All you need is a basket – in and around the hedgerows and woodlands there are plenty of dead and fallen branches that make excellent firewood. Recently dropped branches are good, otherwise look for dead wood that has been held clear of the ground by the branches of a neighbouring tree, as it will be lovely and dry. Don't bother with logs that are covered in moss and have been lying on the ground for a long time, as these will be too damp and no good for burning. Another reason for not collecting such damp wood is that it provides a very important habitat for some of our rarest woodland creatures, such as the stag beetle.

I am lucky enough to have thirty acres of woodland on the farm which we manage, so firewood is never in short supply – any tree that is felled is put to good use. If you are not in such a fortunate position, you can buy wood that has been cut locally from managed woodland. Such services will be advertised in the small ads section of your local paper – you often have to buy a trailer-load, which costs around fifty to a hundred quid, but they will deliver it to your door. If you are not going to use your wood immediately or have a large quantity, you will need to store it properly. Freshly cut timber needs to be kept out of the bad weather so that it can dry out – properly stored, wood will last you for ages. Firewood storage does not have to be a complicated arrangement: all you need to do is keep the rain off, so a simple tarpaulin will do, or a corner of a garage. I keep mine in an old wooden shed.

Building a fire to cook on

Building a fire to cook on is all about starting small and working your way up in stages. Preparation is everything – there is no point even striking a match until you have all your wood ready and in the right order. Having things organized and to hand means there is no need to rush off and fetch missing items – this is very important, as you should never leave a fire unattended for any length of time. To get the fire under way you will need some form of kindling: this is basically any material that is easily combustible, such as shreds of paper, small twigs or dry grass. One of the best things to use is splinters of soft wood such as pine. You can cut your own, or buy it – it's available in bags from most petrol stations, already cut. I split these down further so that I end up with three piles of sticks ranging from small to medium and large, the thinnest being the thickness of a pencil. Once I get the thinnest sticks going I begin to add the thicker ones until I graduate up to the firewood proper. Don't be in too much of a rush to add your larger pieces of wood, otherwise you may be in danger of overloading the fire and smothering the flames. Fire needs a good supply of oxygen as well as fuel to burn properly, so it's important not to pack the wood or fuel too tightly. You can increase the flow of oxygen by blowing on the glowing embers, which will cause them to glow intensely and spread. Continue blowing until flames appear.

Cooking over a fire

We all have memories of barbecues where we have been given charcoaled chicken still raw in the middle, but food cooked properly over a real fire has a quality all of its own. It comes alive and gains a new dimension, with a mellow smoky flavour that intensifies the natural qualities of the food being cooked. Cooking on an electric or gas hob is fine, but you can never compare it to an open fire – there is something about cooking outside that's fun and feels natural and healthy. Most people probably think cooking on an open fire is far beyond their abilities, but it isn't – there's no major difference from cooking on a charcoal barbecue. The key to cooking over an open fire or barbecue is not to rush things, or be over-eager to get the food on. You must let the flames die down – you don't want the raging heat of a fire that is just getting going, you are after the more even and controlled heat from a mature fire. Before you use your fire for cooking you want it to burn clean, which means that the majority of smoke has cleared and the flames have died down, so that you are left with lovely hot glowing embers.

You need to prevent direct contact between the fire and the food that you are cooking, otherwise you will end up with a charred lump. There are a number of ways to prevent this and to achieve more control of the cooking process: you can either cook the food on a spit over the fire, or wrap the food in a protective covering, such as foil, and place it on the embers. More simply, you can set up a grill over the fire, which is great for cooking steaks, sausages and burgers. It also gives you a sturdy platform to put pots and pans on, to boil water, make stews or fry onions. I have a fantastic-looking Jamaican clay pot that I plonk on the grill over an open fire and cook all sorts of things in. It really comes into its own in late autumn, when we begin to clear out the vegetable garden and build bonfires that burn away as we work. As they begin to burn down I get my trusty pot and put in the odd pheasant, a couple of onions, a few spuds and a canful of beer, and let the whole thing bubble away for a few hours. I can tell you, after all that hard work on those cold days it's like having a steaming pot of heaven to look forward to! The easiest way to build a grill is by stacking up a few old bricks or building blocks to fit your grill and building your fire inside. Make sure the blocks or bricks are level and sturdy, so they won't tumble over.

To demonstrate some different cooking methods, both for the open fire and for the barbecue, I've included a few recipes that have worked really well for me. The thing that is important about them is how they are cooked – what you cook is up to you and your imagination.

Baked Trout in Cider-soaked Newspaper

This is a great way to cook fish on a fire if you don't have a griddle or pan. You can use foil, but it can easily tear and you can end up with your dinner in flames. This method is fantastic as it not only bakes but steams, so you capture all the lovely flavours as well as keeping the fish moist, which can be a real problem when cooking it over a fire. The idea is to wrap the fish in a good layer of well-soaked newspaper, which acts as a fireproof blanket and stops the trout from burning. You need at least 10 sheets of newspaper (don't use waxy paper). Soak them to the point of tearing – I add more flavour by using either cider or a bottle of cheap white wine to soak the paper, but you can just use water if you like.

Unless the trout is a large one, you really need one fish per person. Once the fish is gutted and washed, fill the cavity with smashed garlic and lemon thyme and roll the whole thing up tightly in the dampened newspaper, making sure you fold in the ends. It pays to secure the package with some string. You should now have a neat, well-soaked parcel ready to put into the fire. Carefully place it on a flat pile of embers and leave it to cook, turning occasionally. The heat will begin to evaporate the moisture in the paper, steaming the fish and preventing the parcel from bursting into flames.

Once the paper begins to blacken it's time to take the whole thing out of the fire before it gets too dry and catches light – have a glass of water handy just in case you need to give it a bit of a dousing. Cut the string, slowly unwrap the fish and serve steaming hot. I always find a good spot to sit and eat it straight out of the paper – which has to be one of life's great luxuries. When I'm done, everything left over goes on the fire, so no washing up!

This method is equally successful in a domestic oven – use 2 sheets of newspaper (broadsheet) and bake for about 20 minutes at 180°C/350°F/gas mark 4, checking occasionally that the paper isn't charring too much.

Mussels Cooked in a Sack

If you live near the coast you should be able to collect your own mussels at low tide. However, only do this if you are confident that the waters around your particular part of the coastline are relatively clean. Try to avoid any area close to a drainage water outlet, as mussels are filter feeders and can build up levels of contaminants.

Fill two containers with sea water, and put the mussels you've collected into one of them to transport them home. Leave the other one mussel-free. When you get home, put the whole container of mussels into the fridge overnight, stirring occasionally. Next day you will find that the mussels have expelled their waste and grit, so pour the old water away and transfer the mussels into your second container of sea water. Put them back in the fridge for one more day, after which their systems will be thoroughly flushed and they'll be ready for eating.

If collecting your own mussels is not an option, you can buy them fresh from all good fishmongers. They are great value for money. You need around 1kg/2lb 3oz of mussels for two people, but if you are going to cook mussels like this you really want to do it when you have a few friends round, just because it is so spectacular. Before cooking you will need to clean your mussels. First rinse them in clean fresh water, removing and discarding any that are open, and give the remaining mussels a good scrub to remove any dirt and barnacles. The mussel's beard can easily be removed by pinching it between your finger and thumb and pulling it to one side – if this proves too difficult, use the back of a knife for a bit more leverage.

For this recipe you need one of those old-fashioned hessian sacks that potatoes used to come in, or those used to carry coffee beans. You can still buy them from most hardware shops – they sell them for use as sandbags. Once you get the sack home, give it a good wash in clean water, turning it inside out to make sure all dust and unwanted materials are expelled. Once your sack is clean, put in your mussels, tie up the end and dunk the whole thing into fresh water. Allow most of the water to drip off before laying it on to the hot embers of the fire. Once on the hot fire it will begin to hiss as the water turns to steam, cooking the mussels. They only need 10 minutes or so until they are done and before the sack dries out too much. Get yourself a nice big clean surface, such as a table-top, open the sack, tip the whole lot out, then sit round and tuck in!

Whole Roast Chicken with Rosemary and Thyme Butter

Any meat can be cooked over the open fire or barbecue, but the key to success is matching the cut to the method. For example, there is no point trying to cook a large shoulder of pork on a simple barbecue, as all you will end up with is a piece of meat that is black on the outside and red raw on the inside. What you want is a cut of meat that will cook evenly without charring or drying out. Unless slowly spit-roasted, a whole chicken would seem impractical to cook on an open fire or barbecue. However, with a few simple modifications, cooking a whole chicken on the open fire becomes simple and straightforward. What you need to do is to flatten it out so it becomes wider and thinner, a process known as butterflying which you can ask your butcher to do for you.

Serves 4

Strip the leaves from 2 or 3 sprigs of rosemary and a good bunch of thyme, roughly chop them and put them into a clean mixing bowl. Add 115g/4oz of butter and begin to knead in the chopped herbs. Once everything is well mixed, mould the herb butter into a ball. If not needed immediately, wrap it in clingfilm and refrigerate.

Take the butterflied chicken and slip your fingers under the skin at the neck end of the bird, separating the skin from the breasts. Make your way over to the legs and do the same there, taking care not to tear the skin. Now take a handful of herbed butter and spread it evenly over the chicken under the skin – any left over can be spread over the outside of the bird, along with a little salt and freshly ground black pepper. Grill the chicken over the hot embers of the fire or the hot coals of the barbecue for around half an hour, or until the juices run clear. To ensure even cooking, turn the bird every 5 or 6 minutes.

Spit-roasting

This has to be the ultimate in outdoor cooking – visually dramatic, it's a real bit of food theatre. Spit-roasts are associated with times of celebration; they conjure up images of medieval feasts, with whole oxen or pigs being slowly turned over a blazing fire. Spit-roasting has seen a real revival, with hog roast becoming an essential part of any party or public gathering, from village fêtes to music festivals. Their popularity has increased so much that I know of one guy in Hampshire who has started to keep pigs specially to supply his own hog-roasting business. I love the whole event of a hog roast, the preparation, the anticipation as it slowly cooks, right up to the eating. A whole pig cooked on a spit is a wonderful thing, but for most of us it isn't the most practical thing to prepare or cook. In case you've been anxious that I might be going to get you to wrestle with a huge pig in one hand and a large skewer in the other, you can stop worrying. You don't have to have a whole pig to create this spectacle. There are some great ways to spit-roast that are easy to prepare, cook quickly and are fantastic when you have a few mates round.

Spit-roasted Stuffed Salmon

This is an ingenious method of roasting a salmon, or any large fish where the preparation is essential to the recipe's success. The key to the whole thing, because you are going to stuff the salmon, is how the fish is gutted. A fish that has been gutted in the conventional way will result in all the stuffing and juices dropping out as the whole thing is turned. You can sew the opening closed, but the flesh of fish easily tears, especially when cooked. What you are after is a fish that has had its innards removed from the head end rather than by cutting open the belly. You can ask your fishmonger to do this, or you can buy a fish that hasn't been cleaned and do it yourself – don't worry, it isn't as complicated as it sounds.

Preparing your fish

Hook your finger under the gills and pull out the gills and as much of the guts as possible. Use a spoon to extract the remaining fish innards, then rinse the inside of the fish thoroughly under a tap and set aside to dry while you prepare the stuffing.

Heat a pan and fry the bacon until crisp, then add the onion, garlic and mushrooms and cook until until the onions are softened. Add the other ingredients and mix well.

Cooking the fish

Push the stuffing into the hole created under the gills, a little at a time – the last thing you want to do is damage the fish at this point. Use the handle of a wooden spoon or something similar to push the stuffing all the way down until the cavity is filled. Secure the fish to the spit by passing it through the fish's mouth and out through its tail, then attach the holding forks to the spit. Cut a length of butcher's string around five times the length of your fish. Find the middle of the string and tie it around the holding fork at the tail end. Wind the free ends of the string around the fish several times in a criss-cross pattern until you reach the head, then secure the string by tying it to the holding fork at the head end. Now your fish is safely fastened,

A 1.4kg/3lb fish serves 6–8

For the stuffing

- 5 rashers of streaky bacon, chopped
- 1 onion, chopped
- 2 cloves of garlic
- 4 big mushrooms, chopped
- 3 slices of bread, made into breadcrumbs
- 2 eggs
- salt and freshly ground black pepper
- ½ a glass of white wine
- a handful of chopped fresh parsley

position your spit over the fire fairly close to the hot embers but not so close that it will catch fire. A large fish with stuffing will take some cooking, and you should really be looking at 10 to 12 minutes per 450g/1lb. When cooked, the flesh should come away from the bone with ease. If the fire begins to get a little too fierce and the skin of the fish starts to burn, don't panic: either move the spit higher up or give the fire a little douse of water.

Once it's cooked, transfer the whole thing to a large serving dish – if you haven't got one, a big tray or a clean work surface will do. Cut off the string, undo the holding forks and slowly withdraw the spit very carefully. Cut the skin down the fish's back from its head to its tail and then do the same along the belly – you only want to separate the skin, so be careful not to cut too deep. Now with a knife pull the skin away from the fish to reveal the beautiful pink flesh underneath. Divide the exposed salmon into two main fillets by drawing the blade along the line of the spine – the flesh can then be easily removed by easing it away from the backbone with a knife set at a low angle. Serve up the salmon with a good spoonful of stuffing and a wedge of lemon, and sit back and enjoy your labours.

Spit-roasted Barbecued Rack of Sticky Ribs

This has got to be one of my favourite finger-foods. Pork ribs are cheap to buy, and as they are relatively thin and flat they cook very well on an open fire or a barbecue. You can cook them as single ribs, and most butchers sell them this way, although I like to cook my ribs intact. I find this way the meat stays moist and makes the cooking a whole lot easier, plus they look spectacular when you carve them at the table. Some butchers will lift the ribs out by cutting round the bones, leaving the meat still attached to the loin or belly, especially if they intend to cure it for bacon. Others tend to go for the easier and time-saving option of removing the whole section of ribs in one sheet, and it is this that you are after. Ask your butcher to prepare ribs like this for you, but give him a little notice.

Serves 4

Before cooking I marinate the ribs for around 2 hours in the fridge. If you have a number of racks you can build a rib sandwich, with racks of ribs stacked on top of each other and your marinate in between, turning them every half-hour. You can use anything you like to marinate as long as it has a sugary quality, as this will caramelize during cooking, giving that wonderful sticky quality. You can buy prepared barbecue sauces, but some of the mass-produced brands can taste too artificial. I use a jar of the world-famous Jules and Sharpie chilli jam – these two mad ladies still make this wonderful creation at home in their kitchen. You can find them at Borough Market, where they share a pitch with Sillfield Farm once a month, as well as in a few select outlets (see Useful Addresses, page 314). A very good alternative to buying a marinade is to make your own – my favourites are a combination of honey and mustard, and a spicy tomato sauce (see the Spicy Chicken Supper recipe on page 66).

Once marinated, the rack of ribs can be threaded on to a spit and roasted. Baste them frequently and generously with more of the marinade to ensure maximum stickiness. The ribs need to be cooked slowly so that they don't dry out too quickly, and this is where the marinade comes in, as it helps to protect the meat's natural juices. Depending on the heat of your fire the ribs should take around 45 minutes to cook – they will be ready to eat when the juices run clear.

Fireside cooking

A very basic way to cook over an open fire is that iconic campfire method of slowly roasting your food over the hot embers, skewered on the end of a large stick. It's a lovely way to cook, a real must at any Bonfire Night party, sitting round the glowing warmth of the fire chatting with a few mates. The heat thrown off is amazing – you only have to feel the front of your legs after a few minutes. The sides of the fire are fantastic for cooking foods that don't require such intense heat – place them around the edge of the fire on wooden boards, or on sticks stuck into the ground, and leave them to roast slowly. You can easily move the food closer to the heat or further away, depending on the temperature and speed you want to cook at. Here are a few great things you can cook next to the fire.

Mini Pigs in Blankets

Pigs in blankets are simply sausages wrapped in streaky bacon. They are usually cooked alongside the turkey at Christmas, but they are fantastic at any time. They can be cooked on skewers like the prawns on page 165. I use chipolatas, as they cook more quickly – if you can't get them you can use regular sausages but they will take a little longer.

Serves 4

Take the rind off your streaky bacon if you have not already bought it rindless. Take a rasher, lay it flat on a board and, holding the blade almost flat to the board, run a knife along the bacon. This stretches the rasher and makes it easier to wrap round the sausage. Wind a rasher around your sausage or chipolata until the whole length is covered. Cut off any excess bacon, fasten with a cocktail stick at each end, then pass a wooden kebab skewer down the length of the sausage. Stick the skewers in the ground and let the pigs in blankets cook for around 15 minutes, until the bacon is golden brown and the sausagemeat is thoroughly cooked.

Prawns on Sticks

Prawns are great for this because they cook relatively quickly and have a protective shell, or exoskeleton, that prevents the juicy flesh inside from burning and drying out. Eel also cooks very well this way.

Allow 3 large prawns per person

To skewer your prawns, which should be in the shell, you will need a bunch of those wooden kebab skewers that you can get at most hardware shops and supermarkets. Taking a prawn in one hand and a skewer in the other, slowly push the sharp end of the stick into the prawn just under its eyes. Now run the skewer through the whole length of the prawn until the tip reaches the end of its tail. Place the other end of the skewer firmly in the ground, at a slight angle, next to the fire and leave to cook slowly, turning every few minutes. Depending on how close your skewer is to the fire, a large prawn should be cooked within 10 minutes or so – it's done when it has turned that beautiful characteristic pink colour, with a lovely crispy shell. Remember the prawns will be hot, so let them cool before you tuck in (though they are so irresistible I always end up with burnt fingers).

Fish on Boards

Whole fish can be cooked at the fire's edge by flattening them out, kipper-style, and nailing them to a wooden board which is then propped up by a log or a few bricks in front of the fire. The best fish to use are sardines and mackerel because they are oily fish and won't dry out during the slow cooking process.

Allow 1 large or 2 smaller fish per person

Take the fish and trim off the fins – if you are using herrings you will have to scale them if your fishmonger has not done it already. Cut off the head with a sharp knife, and if the fish has not been cleaned, make a slit along its belly and remove the guts. Open it out, at the same time slipping your thumbs under the backbone and running them the length of the fish to lift out the backbone and ribs. When you get to the base of the tail, cut the backbone, with ribs attached, away with a pair of scissors. Any remaining bones can be lifted out with tweezers if necessary. Get yourself a clean plank of wood or an old wooden chopping board and place the fish on it skin side down. Hammer a few nails around the flattened fish to secure them – not too deep, just enough so that they can be pulled out by wiggling them backwards and forwards a few times. Place the fish close to the edge of the fire, propped up at a 45° angle. The fish at the top of the board will cook slower than those at the bottom, so flip the whole thing round every 5 or 10 minutes. The fish will be cooked in about half an hour – the flesh should come away easily with a fork. Pull the nails out of the board (be careful not to burn your fingers) and serve with plenty of cracked black pepper and a wedge of lemon.

Hot ashes

Once the fire has died down all you are left with is a bed of ashes, and despite the lack of flame this final stage of the fire offers some of the best cooking opportunities. The ash remains extremely hot for a long period of time, with a fairly consistent heat that's ideal for cooking. I have often returned to the remains of fires I've cooked on the previous day only to find that the ash was still very hot. Gently brush away the top layer of ash to reveal the hidden glowing embers, and with a little blowing and a bundle of kindling you can soon transform them into a blazing fire again. It's a godsend when you're camping and you're desperate for that morning cup of tea! The only problem with cooking in hot ash is preventing it getting all over your food, but this is easily overcome with the use of a little foil. Potatoes wrapped in foil have to be the classic ash-cooked food – whenever my dad had a bonfire in autumn we always used to wrap three or four potatoes in foil, push them into the heart of the fire and leave them to cook in the ashes. I still remember the plumes of steam rising up into the cold air as the potatoes were unwrapped. Potatoes are great cooked like this, but with a little imagination and some experimentation you will soon find there is a whole range of foods that benefit from ash-baking. Here are a few of my specials for those nights round the campfire.

Foil-baked Camembert

This is basically like a mini fondue, lots of calories but worth every single one. You can always take the stairs rather than the lift next day at work!

Serves 2 as a starter

What you want is a whole cheese in its little box, such as a Somerset Camembert. Before cooking, lift the cheese from its box, remove any plastic wrapping, and place the naked cheese back in its box with the lid on top. Now wrap the whole thing in foil and bury it in the hot ashes for 15 minutes. When the time's up, remove the foil and open the box to reveal the hot melted cheese – the skin should still be intact, so with a knife cut a circle round the top and lift it off. I just tear chunks of good crusty bread and dunk them into the melted cheese, or you can spread it with a knife. Whatever, do it fast – it will not stay melted for long. Mind you, that has never been a problem when I've cooked this – there's usually a long queue of people with bread in their hands!

Marrow Stuffed with Sausagemeat

This is something I came up with when I started to get into growing my own vegetables and found myself with too many marrows. Michaela is fantastic in the vegetable garden – she's a great planner, and as a result she achieves what she sets out to do. I tend to have a general plan, but I can be somewhat erratic and act on impulse. I recently went to visit a lady just outside Saffron Walden to buy three peacocks, but while I was there a few other things caught my eye. When I got back to the farm, as well as the three peacocks I also had thirty chickens, three ducks, six doves, eight quails and two kittens. The same thing happened with the marrow – I was driving along and came across a lot of young marrow plants for sale. They were cheap, so I filled the truck with as many as I could. A few months later I found myself trying to eat marrow with everything and anything, and as a result I discovered this fantastic recipe. It's a great way to use a marrow whole. I love to bring it to the table for serving in all its glory, like a roast.

Serves 4

• 1 medium marrow

For the stuffing
• 30g/1oz butter
• 1 small onion, finely chopped
• 225g/8oz sausagemeat
• 4 tomatoes, skinned, deseeded and chopped
• 50g/2oz white breadcrumbs
• 2 tablespoons chopped fresh parsley
• salt and freshly ground black pepper
• 1 egg, lightly beaten

Cut the marrow in half lengthways and scoop out the seeds. Melt the butter in a pan and gently fry the onion until soft but not coloured. Add the sausagemeat, stirring to break it up, and cook until browned. Add the tomatoes and cook for 5 minutes. Remove from the heat, add the breadcrumbs, parsley, salt and freshly ground black pepper, and mix in the egg to bind.

Spoon the stuffing into the two halves of the marrow. Tie the halves together with string and wrap in buttered foil. Cook in the hot coals of your barbecue for about an hour. Alternatively, you can cook it in a conventional oven for 1 hour at 180°C/350°F/gas mark 4.

Baked Oranges in Rum

This is one of those recipes that are so simple but have a combination of flavours that blow you away – the thought of these taste time-bombs as I write this has already got my mouth watering.

Use 1 orange per person

The general rule of thumb is the thicker the skin the sweeter the orange. Once you have your orange, get a small knife and slice the top and bottom off so it doesn't roll around. With your orange standing upright, slice down the sides to remove the peel and pith. Do the same for all your oranges. I keep the peel in the freezer and pull it out to use in other dishes that require a little bit of zest – it's great for making warm fruit punches with.

Before I do any more to the oranges I get my foil sorted by cutting it into even squares and stacking them in a pile shiny side down. Each square of foil should be big enough to completely cover the whole fruit. Slice your orange crosswise into thick slices (around 1.5cm), and at this point get rid of any remaining piths and pips. Now what you want to do is basically reassemble the sliced orange in the middle of a sheet of foil, but in between each layer sprinkle brown sugar and a little cinnamon. Gather up the foil around the orange, leaving enough room to pour in a good splash of rum (this is a great recipe for finishing off those bottles of booze at the back of the cupboard that were given to you as holiday presents). With the orange well doused, close the package by gathering up the foil at the top and twisting it together to form a tuft. Using a small shovel, bury the parcels around 10cm deep in hot ashes, making sure the tufts are upright and exposed, as you don't want any ash getting in – or worse, any rum getting out. Give them a good 15 minutes in the ash before lifting them out. Carefully open up the foil parcels, lift out the orange segments, arrange them on a plate and spoon the hot sweet rum over the top.

Bananas and Vanilla Sugar

I love cooked bananas. They're not the most sophisticated dish, but I don't care, it's the stuff of childhood dreams, the taste and mushy texture of that soft sweet banana that just melts in the mouth, a moment of real indulgence.

Use 1 banana per person

To start off you need a medium ripe banana for each person, nice and yellow but not too soft. Interestingly, if you place unripe fruit in a bowl with ripe bananas it will soon ripen, due to the gas given off by the bananas. With a sharp knife nick the skin of the banana and run the point of the blade lengthways round the fruit until you join up to the start point, trying not to cut into the flesh. Peel off the top half of the banana skin, leaving the bottom half still on the fruit.

Place each banana on a square sheet of foil and sprinkle the exposed fruit with a good layer of vanilla sugar. Enclose the banana by bringing both ends of the foil together and folding them down, forming a tight crease, and do the same to the sides to form a sealed parcel. Take the banana parcels and bury them in a good 2 to 3 inches of hot ash for 20 minutes, after which they should be piping hot. Carefully unwrap the foil and serve the bananas in their skins, which look like little bent canoes, with a healthy scoop of good ice cream.

How to make vanilla sugar

Vanilla sugar is so easy to make and such a useful store-cupboard ingredient. Simply get a largish, clean jar and fill it nearly to the top with caster sugar. Take a vanilla pod and stick it into the middle of the sugar, burying it to the top. Leave it for at least 2 days before using, during which time the delicious vanilla flavour will permeate the sugar.

Use in desserts, biscuits, cakes, drinks (although it's not too good in tea) – in fact let your imagination run wild!

Top up the jar with new sugar as you use the vanilla-flavoured store and you will always have some to hand.

Catherine Wheel Sausages

This is basically a large sausage wrapped round to form a coil. The most common sausage you will find in this shape is the traditional Cumberland, or you can ask your butcher to run you off a long sausage without any links.

A 340g/12oz sausage serves 2

Coil your sausage into a tight ring, secure it with two wooden kebab skewers, and barbecue it on both sides until golden brown. When it's done, remove it to a large plate, take out the skewers and cut it as if you were slicing a cake, giving each person a wedge of juicy sausage. At the farm we produce a coiled sausage we call the Essex Love Sausage, so named because of its aphrodisiac ingredients. To tell you the truth, it was originally created in an attempt to sell more sausage. As we sold it by the inch, the idea was that when offered either a three-inch or a seven-inch love sausage the customer was more likely to leave with the larger! Obviously you can tell that this brilliant marketing ploy was aimed at our male customers. However, I must say it is now one of our best-sellers!

Boiling water

If you're camping for any length of time you will need a source of hot water at some point, either for washing yourself, for making a cup of coffee or for doing the dishes. The most common way to boil water on a campsite is usually in a metal can or camping kettle on the stove or over the fire. It's all extra baggage to carry, but I've found an amazing way to boil water in its plastic bottle. I discovered it when I was backpacking in Australia and got chatting in a bar to a guy who worked on a nearby sheep station. These guys have to spend long periods of time out in the bush and have to be very self-sufficient. He told me how they made campfire bread and boiled water in this very unusual way. I left the bar thinking it was impossible, and that he must have been having me on, or had had too much to drink. Nevertheless, the idea of heating water in a plastic bottle placed in the middle of a log fire kept coming back to me. Was it possible? I had to give it a go.

I made a good fire and followed the method explained to me by the guy in the bar. I got two large plastic water bottles, removed the caps, stood them upright in the centre of the blaze and waited. The first bottle buckled slightly and fell over – the water poured out causing a cloud of steam and the bottle was no more. At that point all I could think of was that Aussie and how he must have laughed as I left the bar, knowing that at some point I would be trying to attempt the impossible. As I stared into the fire, trying to come to terms with being so gullible, I noticed that the other bottle was still standing – and what was more, there were small bubbles rising up to the top. It was working. The way it works is quite simple: at first the plastic is prevented from melting due to the cooling effect of the water inside. However, as the water temperature rises to boiling point it loses this cooling ability, and the bottle buckles and melts – the trick is to catch it just before it boils. It has to be seen to be believed – a real party trick!

Barbecuing

Obviously not everyone is able to have an open log fire in their backyard, but most of us can have a barbecue, no matter how small. For me, barbecue cooking gives just as much exhilaration as cooking on an open fire, and you can easily use most of the recipes and cooking methods described on the previous pages. Whenever the sun shows its face for more than ten minutes I start planning what I am going to cook on the barbie. I have two small clay barbecues with a simple grill that fits over a bowl-like structure – the charcoal sits in this and as it burns the ash is collected in the bottom. It is very simple, but it does the job without flashy chrome lids, side burners, temperature gauges and all the other things barbecue manufacturers try to tell us are essential. I don't see the point in buying one of those barbecues that has everything – it defeats the object, and you might as well rip out the cooker in the kitchen and install it in the garden. Gas barbecues are good in that they are easy to start and you have control over the output of heat during cooking, but I miss the smoky flavour that charcoal brings to the food. You can buy a charcoal barbecue very cheaply, or you can convert almost any object into a barbecue from a metal bucket to an old oil drum as long as it's fireproof. An alternative is to build a more permanent structure out of bricks.

When buying charcoal it is very important that you purchase only from a sustainable source. I buy mine locally in Suffolk from Osier Farm, who make their charcoal from their own coppice woodland. This is great, as not only is it local and sustainable but it also ensures that the ancient method of coppicing, which is so important in sustaining woodland biodiversity, continues. This charcoal is more expensive, but you get what you pay for. British charcoal produced in a sustainable manner is streets ahead of the cheap imported rubbish, which is made from the unwanted timber left after large-scale deforestation – the same deforestation that has helped accelerate so many of the environmental problems that now affect us all.

The key to cooking on the barbecue, as with an open log fire, is to let the flames burn down first and cook on the hot embers; you want the charcoal to turn from sooty black to a greyish white. Barbecuing has now become part of our culture, so much so that many cookbooks have been published on the subject and during the summer the supermarket shelves are fully stocked with cold beers and special barbecue packs. There are heaps of things you can cook on the humble barbecue, but simplicity is the key to success. However, simple doesn't mean boring, and to prove this I've included some of my favourite, very simple but effective recipes.

Sweetcorn in Their Jackets

Cooking sweetcorn still enclosed in its green leafy jacket works in two ways.
First, it prevents the yellow cob from burning and blistering, and second,
the moisture retained by the covering creates steam, which keeps the corn
wonderfully juicy.

Use 1 cob per person

To prevent the moisture escaping it's a good idea to tie the top of the green leaves
of the husk together with a piece of string. Put the sweetcorn on a hot grill and turn
regularly until the husks are dark brown all over. When cooked remove the husk
carefully, as it will be piping hot, cover the whole cob with lashings of butter and serve.

T-Bone

Any steak is great on the barbecue, but I prefer the T-bone because the
bone helps to give it a little more tenderness on the grill. I cook my steak
on a high heat to seal it on both sides, then move it to the side of the grill,
where the heat is a little less fierce, to finish it off.

A 450g/1lb steak serves 2

Before you put your T-bone on the barbie you will see a piece of meat that hangs down
a bit like a tail – wrap this round the smaller fillet section of the steak and secure it
with a couple of cocktail sticks. Once cooked, remove the steak and leave it to rest on
a carving board for 5 minutes or so. Take out the cocktail sticks, cut off the tail of the
steak, and cut round the T-bone to free both the fillet and the sirloin section. Carve
thinly across the grain and serve in overlapping slices on a large plate with a good
dollop of homemade horseradish (see page 111 for recipe).

Rosemary Kebabs

I've nicked this idea from my mate Jamie – he does a version using Italian mozzarella, but I've changed it slightly by using home-cured streaky bacon and British goat's cheese. Hope you don't mind, J!

This is a great way to use rosemary, and it looks and tastes fantastic. Basically the idea is to use long straight twigs of rosemary as kebab skewers, which can then be loaded with a whole combination of goodies. Don't feel you have to follow my recipe exactly – you can put whatever you want on your kebabs.

Cut the bread into 2.5cm/1inch cubes and put them into a bowl. Strip the lower leaves off the rosemary stems and add to the bowl with enough olive oil to drench the bread. Crush the garlic and add to the mix along with the sea salt and black pepper. Mix well and set aside for the moment.

Roll pieces of the goat's cheese into little balls about the size of walnuts. Take a rasher of streaky bacon about 3–4cm/1¼ –1¾ inches long and carefully wrap it around each piece of cheese.

Cut the sausages into 1.5cm/¾ inch pieces.

Now you can make the kebabs. Start with a cube of bread, followed by a piece of sausage, then by the cheese wrapped in bacon, and continue until everything is used up.

Grill or barbecue over a medium heat for about 15 to 20 minutes, or until the sausages are cooked through.

Serves 4

- 1 stale loaf of bread or French sticks
- 4 straight rosemary twigs, 30cm/12 inches long
- a couple of good glugs of olive oil
- 5 cloves of garlic
- sea salt
- cracked black pepper
- 8 small cubes of soft goat's cheese
- 4–6 rashers of streaky bacon
- a couple of meaty sausages

More ways of cooking outside

Outdoor cooking isn't just confined to the campfire or barbecue – all over the world different cultures have developed ingenious ways of cooking their food outside, from building elaborate clay ovens to cooking in a covered pit of hot sand. Once you have mastered cooking over the open fire and exhausted all the possibilities on the barbecue you may want to experiment with alternative ways of cooking. Here are a few ideas to get you started – they will take a little preparation, but they are great fun.

Dustbin oven

The dustbin oven is a great way to roast a whole bird or joint of meat. It looks a bit bizarre but it really works. This way of cooking is used all over the world in many different forms, but the basic idea is to place a large metal container over a fire, creating a makeshift oven. I built my first outdoor oven on my eighteenth birthday. I spent the early morning with a few mates getting everything prepared, and just as we were finishing the kebabs and slicing the hot dog rolls, one of my friends suggested that it would be awesome if we roasted a whole chicken outside. We all put our heads together to decide on our plan, then set off to raid my dad's shed for anything suitable for building an oven. After half an hour of mass rummaging, we ended up with an old parrot's cage and a sheet of flexible metal of some description. The idea was to hang the chicken from a meat hook inside the cage, wrap the metal round the outside and put the whole thing on to a fire sunk into a pit. It sounded foolproof to us, but unfortunately it wasn't. We put the oven over the fire pit and things were going fine as we smugly sat back with some cold beers, basking in our success. Suddenly to our horror the whole thing began to melt – great lumps of metal were dripping everywhere, until all that remained was the naked skeleton of the parrot's cage with a sooty uncooked chicken hanging inside. We soon discovered that my mate Andy Slade, who had discovered the fabulous flexible metal used to wrap round the cage, had in fact grabbed a sheet of old roofing lead. We quickly decided to put it down to experience, and needless to say there were very few takers for our lead-studded roast chicken!

I am much better at building outdoor ovens these days, and one of the best things to use is an old-fashioned metal dustbin. If you don't have one you can still buy them from most hardware stores relatively cheaply. Give your bin a good scrub, wash it out with soapy water and leave it to dry while you start work on your fire. You can either dig out a fire pit or build a raised one out of bricks or concrete blocks, it all depends on your situation and what suits you. Whatever design you decide to go for, the fire pit needs to be at least a foot deep, with an inside area measuring one foot by two and a half. The bin should be laid on its side and fit comfortably over the pit, with a good amount of space between the fire and the side of the bin. If the bin is too close, or touching the fire, it will either scorch the metal or smother the flames, putting it out. Remember, the fire needs room to breathe.

Wood or charcoal or a combination of both is fine to use as fuel, the important thing is to get a good quantity of hot embers going. I always add some of those coal-like barbecue briquettes, as they are relatively slow-burning and give a more consistent heat, which is just what is needed. Once your fire is under way and the temperature begins to get hot inside, it's time to add your chicken. Put it in a roasting dish and set the dish in the bin oven on a brick – this helps to keep the dish off the hot metal as well as elevating it to the middle of the oven, helping it cook evenly. Another way to make sure your chicken cooks properly is to sit it upright on its legs, placing an open tin can into its cavity to act as a stable base. Once your chicken is in place, close the lid of the bin – secure it by pushing a stick through the handle at a slight angle and inserting the end into the ground. This will prevent the lid falling off and the oven losing its heat. The cooking time will of course depend on the constancy of the heat produced from the fire, so to make sure your chicken is done, cut it open with a knife – if the juices run clear it's ready.

Pit bake

This is an ancient form of outdoor cooking that spans many cultures across the continents, from the Americas to the South Pacific, but it's the Maoris of New Zealand who have made it famous. I first came across this method of cooking in Fiji during my backpacking days – I was staying on one of the myriad small islands on a scuba-diving trip and was invited to a young couple's wedding reception. To mark the occasion a small pig had been killed and a large pit dug on the beach to cook it in. The whole process started the day before the party, when large stones were placed in the bottom of the pit and a large fire was lit on top of them. Once the fire died down the stones formed a hot-bed. Layers of seaweed and banana leaves were placed on this hot-bed and the pig was placed on top, wrapped in more banana leaves. Then came more leaves and seaweed, and finally more hot stones were piled on top. After all this the whole thing was buried in the sand to cook. It seemed to take ages, and there was no way of checking how the meat was doing – it isn't as simple as lifting the lid of a pot. However, when the time for the great excavation came, the pig was cooked to perfection, bang on time, to be served to the guests.

You can easily copy this style of outdoor cooking, using the same methods but in a much less elaborate fashion. For example, instead of a whole pig you can use a leg of lamb or a whole fish or chicken – smaller items have the benefit of cooking much quicker. You can use seaweed – though wet sacking or newspaper will do just as well – and a few big bunches of herbs can be thrown in for flavour. The key point to the whole operation is remembering where you buried it . . .

Smoking

Smoking has been used for thousands of years to flavour and preserve all kinds of food, especially fish and meat, but it can also be used as a cooking method. People often think smoking can only be carried out by those who have learnt some sort of mystical skill passed down through the generations, or that you need specialized equipment. It's true that commercial smokehouses have developed techniques almost to the point where smoking becomes an art form, but basic smoking is a very simple process. There are two main methods, cold smoking and hot smoking, and both are easily achievable with very little effort. The basic idea of a cold smoke is to add a smoky flavour to food that will be cooked at a later date, such as bacon. Cold smoking is also used to preserve foods such as fish and pork, but this is often combined with some form of salt application, either by dry salting or brining. Hot smoking on the other hand is really a method of cooking, during which the food takes on a delicious smoky quality. Once you have mastered the basic principles you will be hooked, and will soon be trying to smoke everything that isn't tied down!

Cold smoking

This is a great way to flavour sausages, bacon, hams, cheese and fish, and changes the plainest of food into a sumptuous delicacy. Everyone knows the saying about where there's smoke there's fire, but with cold smoking you want all the smoke without the heat of the fire. The best way to achieve this is to have a separate firebox, from which smoke can be funnelled to a container housing the food. You can use an old oil drum as a firebox, or construct one out of brick, and I find those metal bins sold for burning rubbish are fantastic. Not only are they specifically designed to hold a fire, but they also have a lid with a small chimney to funnel the smoke out of. The smokebox can be as simple or as elaborate as you wish, as long as it provides somewhere to store the food and retains enough smoke to flavour the food. Most containers or boxes – an unwanted cupboard or wardrobe, for example – can quickly be adapted to make a smokebox, and I've even seen an old fridge used for smoking.

Once you have your smokebox and firebox, all you need to do is connect the two, and you can do this with a length of piping, making sure the end connected to the firebox is not made from combustible material. Position your smokebox so that it's higher than your firebox, to aid the natural flow of the smoke. To get your smoke going,

you need wood chippings or sawdust soaked in water – when you add these to the fire in the firebox they will steam and start to produce great clouds of smoke. You can use whatever wood you want, but try to go for something that will give you a distinct flavour, like oak or cherry. Avoid any wood that has been treated with varnish or paint, as the fumes will taint your food. If the chippings or sawdust begin to dry out, just add a little more water to douse them down again. How long you leave your food in the smokebox depends on the strength of smoky flavour you require and the size of the item you want to smoke. As a rough guide, something like a few sausages will need a few hours while a whole chicken is best left smoking for the whole day.

Hot smoking

The easiest way to hot smoke is to use a charcoal barbecue with a lid on top – it couldn't be simpler! All you need to do is add wet chippings to the charcoal and cover the barbecue with the lid. The heat from the charcoal will cook the food, while the resulting smoke will give it that delicate but distinctive flavour. Just keep an eye on the chippings to check they are not getting too dry. I used this method recently to smoke a bunch of quails, and the results were fantastic, even though I didn't set out to eat the quails in the first place.

The birds came from a friend who had rescued them from ending up on the menu of a local restaurant (as you read on, this point becomes a little ironic), and I bought them with the idea that they would supply our farm shop with a few eggs as well as adding something different to our growing collection of farmyard fowl. When the birds arrived I installed them in a lovely little run, gave them plenty of feed and fresh water and left them to settle in for the night. However, that night there were other eyes watching over my new little flock. In the morning I was greeted by a scene of carnage – most of the quails had been dragged away, while the remaining birds lay on the ground with fatal bites to the head. Unfortunately for the little birds, a hungry stoat with a family to feed had decided their fate – you can't blame her, she was only doing what was natural.

I believe you should always find something good out of bad, and I was determined not to let these plump little birds go to waste. This may seem a little insensitive, but that's life – to me it would have been a crime not to eat them, and I soon had them cleaned, plucked and oven-ready. I fired up my clay barbecue and waited for the charcoal to burn down until it was white and ashy. Meanwhile I got a good thick bunch of rosemary and submerged it in a bucket of water, and when the charcoal was hot I laid it on top – it let out a great snake-like hiss. On went the grill, then on went the quail, and I placed an upturned terracotta flowerpot over the top to capture all that lovely fragrant smoke. The result was beautifully tender roast quail, golden brown in colour and flavoured throughout by the perfumed rosemary smoke . . . unforgettable!

In the Garden

This chapter is about the wonderful food that can be harvested from your garden or vegetable patch – in fact, even if you're not a gardener there will be something you'll be able to grow. I have written it as a general approach to growing food rather than as a detailed guide, because I think it's fair to say I'm no Alan Titchmarsh but simply a person who loves to grow plants. If you have a large garden or even a modest piece of land you are in a very advantageous position; even if you live in a flat without a balcony you still have a great deal more growing power than you would imagine.

However, before I start getting you to dig up your garden or convert your windowsills into the hanging gardens of Babylon, I want to look at some of the reasons why you should bother in the first place. A friend of mine (who incidentally does now grow a few veggies of his own) once asked me why he should go to all the trouble of growing potatoes when he could buy them cheaply from a supermarket without getting his hands dirty and without all the hard work. It's a very good point: when you work out the labour cost of growing your own vegetables on a small scale it turns out far more costly than the price you can buy them for. If you look at the economics, it would appear to be pointless, although it does depend on what you grow, the scale on which you grow it and the value you place on your own labour. As a farmer I aim to produce food profitably, but on a personal level growing my own food has nothing to do with economics, and I am pleased to say so. It's the economic pressure on farmers to produce cheaper food, from supermarkets and all of us as consumers, that has led to the terrible problems that have occurred in the world's food production.

Growing your own food is all about the quality and flavour of your produce and the peace of mind you achieve from knowing your crops have been grown without the addition of any unwanted chemicals. It is about understanding how food is produced and the effort involved, which in turn gives a greater appreciation of what you eat and how you shop. For example, once you have grown your own tomatoes, the cheap out-of-season Spanish ones will never do again. You will also find yourself wasting less food, as you will soon associate a value with it that goes far beyond money. There is another point too, one I think is the most important of all, something that can never be achieved from buying a bag of spuds from a supermarket. For me it's the reconnection with nature, something we all once shared as children. I always explain the feeling as being a bit like meeting up with an old friend you haven't seen for some time.

I don't expect people to grow all their own food – that's unrealistic, and even I, as a full-time farmer, don't – but if after reading this book you attempt to grow a few lettuces or some herbs I'll feel I have achieved my purpose. Years ago when my grandfather was a young man it was commonplace for people to grow a certain amount of their own food, even if, like my grandparents, they lived in the middle of a city. What they had to spare was swapped with neighbours. Such self-sufficiency was magnified during the Second World War, when in most cities every available green space was turned over to growing food as part of the 'Dig for Victory' campaign. Sadly, only a few urbanites utilize or even realize the resources that they have at their disposal for growing their own food, but this need not be so. Once you start on the road to growing a few vegetables or herbs you will soon be hooked, and you will be surprised how quickly you will increase in growing know-how, and in friends, come harvest time.

Growing in the Garden

My first job when I arrived on the farm was to clear the vegetation that
had overgrown the buildings during the fifteen years they had stood empty.
Cutting down the trees that had grown through the roof of the old tractor
shed and pulling away the creepers that hid part of the old farmhouse really
drove home to me nature's ability to reinstate its equilibrium. You often see
immaculate vegetable gardens where nature appears to be completely under
control. Such gardens usually either employ a whole arsenal of chemicals,
or need a gardener who is so busy weeding that he or she never gets time
to enjoy the results. If you try to fight against nature you may succeed for
a short while but in the end you will lose, a bit like swimming upstream.
It's much better to go with the flow, and to work with the natural balance of
the environment you are in. My vegetable patch is not weed-free, and it often
feels as though I share half my crop with a myriad hungry little creatures
that nibble away at anything green they see. Am I a bad gardener? I'm not
going to win first prize for my leeks, but I am growing food in a way that I
think is right and that gives me enjoyment and results, and for me that's
good enough. You should do what makes you happy and feels right; there
are no hard and fast rules. And don't worry about making mistakes, they're
all part of the learning process – the main thing is just to enjoy yourself.

Natural pest control

If like me you want to grow vegetables and fruit for your own consumption, you will want to avoid using unnatural chemicals to kill off weeds and pests – not only will they contaminate your food, they will also harm other wildlife in the process. However, you need to defend your crops somehow if you are to have a harvest at all.

The natural world will throw at you armies of creatures, such as insects, slugs, snails, that will soon become your sworn enemies. Fortunately there are many other creatures that will serve as your natural allies, and with a little encouragement these will happily come to your aid to wage biological warfare. This is a subject that modern scientists have studied for a number of decades, in the hope of relieving some of the problems faced by agriculture (although it is one Chinese farmers were well versed in some 2,000 years ago, so we would appear to have been somewhat behind the times in the West!). The aim is to encourage into your garden animals that will prey on those determined to eat your crops. You will never completely eradicate your plant pests, but that's not the point – if you did that you would also wipe out the creatures that feed on them. What you need to do is create a balance between prey and predator, and the little damage that does occur to your vegetables is just part of the give and take of maintaining the ecology balance of your patch. Many of these allies will just turn up because there are other creatures to eat. However, you can further increase your ranks of mercenaries by creating natural areas that will act as a refuge during the day and a base from which to mount raids on your garden pests. Such areas can be very simple, for example a pile of logs or a small overgrown strip of grass around your vegetable patch, often referred to as a beetle bank. Biological control using natural predators has become big business, and now you can even buy them by mail order or online and have them delivered to your door ready to release.

Natural allies:

Ladybirds, lacewings, hoverflies, wasps, ground beetles, centipedes, toads, hedgehogs, thrushes and ants.

Companion planting

As soon as humans began to cultivate wild plants and grow them as single crops we created a concentrated food resource, not only for ourselves but also, unwittingly, for every other creature that feeds on such plants. One important way insects detect the plants they feed on is by smell, and if you can disrupt this there is every chance you will be able to prevent severe attacks on your crops. In recent years there has been a lot of research into using plants that release strong odours to protect those more vulnerable to attack. The idea is that such plants release a chemical smokescreen of smell to blanket those released by the plants that the insect is really after. As a result, the attacking insect assumes its favourite food plant is not to be found and flies off to look elsewhere. This is why many gardeners grow rows of chives between crops such as carrots, to prevent attack from carrot root fly. It's known as companion planting, and it's a kind of plant hide-and-seek. Planting your crops in mixed rows has other benefits, too, as you are not presenting insect invaders with large patches of a single type of plant which would otherwise be much easier to detect. Interplanting your vegetables with other plants such as herbs creates a more diverse environment which is better for a balanced ecology. If you plant only one type of crop you will attract only a few types of insects that feed on that plant, and they'll soon become pests. By mixing plants up you create physical barriers that reduce the damage done by pest species. For example, if a cabbage white butterfly keeps landing on or brushing against a different plant, such as rosemary, this hinders its attempts to lay its eggs on your cabbages.

Natural defences

If companion planting or the employment of other creatures to eat your pests does not seem to be working, you may need to beef up your defences. The simplest way is to pay your plants a nightly visit with a torch to collect snails and slugs and a daily one to kill off aphids. Even simply knocking them off the plant they are feeding on will help – studies show that just under half the aphids dislodged from their host plant never make it back on. Another good way to deal with aphids is to spray them with soapy water, which breaks down their waxy outer covering and kills them.

People say that spreading crushed eggshells round lettuces protects them from snails and slugs. I have never found this to be the case and would question the practice, as snails actively search out calcium for their own shell growth. I have found, however, that chilli powder sprinkled round my salad crops does the trick against both slugs and snails – but only when the weather is dry, as the powder is easily washed away by rain.

Give Your Plants What They Need

Like most things in life, pot plants have needs – fulfil them and they will flourish. It always amuses me when my mum complains about her plants not looking as healthy as they did in the garden centre. It is only when I investigate that I discover she hasn't fed them. I explain that, like humans, plants need feeding. If you are going to grow herbs or vegetables in containers you will need to feed them regularly with a liquid feed, otherwise they will soon use up all the available nutrients in their pots and begin to suffer. If on the other hand you are growing your crops on a plot of land, you will need to feed them less often because the plants will have a larger resource of nutrients to draw from. However, after the growing season you will need to use manure to put back the nutrients the plants have removed from the soil. The other essential for good plant growth, one that may sound a bit obvious, is watering, or rather 'correct' watering – water too little or too much and your plants will not thrive. The trick is to water little and often, although during hot weather you may need to water for a little longer. If you water regularly you will soon learn what each crop needs, as you will be inspecting them on a daily basis. Regular watering will also help prevent your plants suffering from extreme environmental conditions brought about by human panic. This is when you have not given your plant enough attention and discover that it is bone dry. Panic and guilt set in and you douse your plant, or if it is growing in a pot you place it in a bucket of water for a day or so, so that the poor plant goes from severe drought conditions to flood in the space of a few days.

When planting your vegetables, make sure they are going to get enough sun. Most will need full exposure, but some may prefer a little protection. When growing plants in pots you will need to turn the pot or container every few days, as the plant will grow towards the sunlight. Failure to do this can lead to uneven growth, and if there are several plants in one pot some may fall behind if they are not getting enough of the sun's rays.

Feeding Your Plants

As well as water and sunshine, your plants need minerals and nutrients, such as nitrogen. These are obtained by the plants from the soil via their root systems, but supplies are not limitless and you need to top up the supply by adding extra plant food to the soil. You can buy various types of plant food from garden centres – they contain manufactured chemicals which will have the desired effect on your plants by increasing their growth. Although these foods are very effective, some are more natural than others. Be careful which you buy, as using chemicals on plants you are going to eat yourself will have its implications. I much prefer to make my own plant food from basic raw materials and produce a wonderful compost.

Manure

Manure makes very good plant food but it has to be well rotted, otherwise the ammonia it contains will actually burn the plants and kill them. At the farm we have a plentiful supply of manure – we have hundreds of pigs, as well as a host of other domestic livestock of every description, each producing a little more with every hour that passes. We pile all the manure from the animals' housing, mixed with their straw bedding, in a large heap at one end of the farm, where we leave it to break down naturally. When it has rotted down sufficiently we dig it into the soil, from which great delights grow.

Now not everyone needs or wants such a large pile of dung, but if you keep livestock you have a plentiful supply of some of the best plant food around. If you are not in a position to keep livestock, it may be a good idea to make friends with someone who does, or ask at your local riding stables, as more often than not they are more than happy for you to take it away. Failing this, you can buy well-rotted manure from garden centres or through ads in your local paper under the gardening section.

Liquid manure

This is a good way to feed your plants on a regular basis. It can be used directly from a watering-can, so the nutrients soak directly into the soil and into the roots of the plants. You can buy manufactured liquid feeds that you dilute in water, but I think making your own is a lot better for the reasons already discussed on the previous page and also because it's a lot cheaper and incredibly easy to do. Making your own liquid feeding system is a great alternative if you don't have enough space for a compost heap. Basically you are trying to create a huge rotting vegetable soup, and many avid gardeners have devised recipes that have become closely guarded secrets, containing things like pigeon droppings and chopped nettles and comfrey. You can make your liquid fertilizer in any waterproof container but I think the best vessel to use is a rainwater butt placed under the downflow pipe from your gutter. This way you have a regular water top-up system and a tap from which you can decant your concoction. If your solution becomes too rich, water it down before you pour it on to your plants.

Compost

Compost usually conjures up images of huge piles of steaming dung swarming with flies and stinking out the neighbourhood, but that couldn't be further from the truth. Composting is the coolest kind of recycling around, and a way for everyone to do their bit for the environment. However, a compost heap shouldn't be seen as your personal refuse tip, it is more like cooking a great meal. You need to add ingredients in the right quantities, and cook slowly, stirring occasionally. You might think that cooking and stirring is taking it a bit far, but it will make perfect sense later! It is safe to say that compost heaps are definitely not rubbish! To me, as someone who is concerned about the environment and as a food producer, composting makes perfect sense. I make a great effort to ensure that the animals I eat are fed decent food, so it would be crazy not to do the same for the crops I grow. Composting also gives you an understanding of the part we can all play in maintaining the ecological balance both on a local scale and worldwide. It's one big relationship – we feed the plants and the plants feed us, and happily round and round we go!

So how does composting work? Basically what you are trying to achieve is a mixture of green waste constructed in such a way that natural decomposition can take place. Natural waste material breaks down, releasing the nutrients within and forming a soil-like structure. It is exactly the same process that happens naturally in habitats such as a woodland floor, where fallen leaves are broken down by a host of small animals, bacteria and fungi to form a rich loamy soil. To start your own heap going you will need somewhere to keep it (any corner of the garden will do) and a compost container (many councils now provide them for free, or you can build one, as I do, out of four wooden pallets tied together with bale string). Having a series of these containers makes the process a lot easier, as it allows you to transfer material from one to another, mixing it all up and speeding up the decomposition process.

Fill up your compost container with vegetable waste from the kitchen and the vegetable patch, as well as any garden waste such as dead leaves and weeds such as nettles. You can add grass clippings, but they need to be well mixed because if they are introduced in large quantities on a regular basis they will prevent air getting in and the whole thing will become an acrid slimy mess. Once you have got a good pile of mixed green waste, the composting process will get going. Bacteria will be the first to start working on the plant matter – as they build up numbers and their activity increases, the heap will generate a serious amount of heat and can reach temperatures well over 100°F (this is the cooking part). You should allow your compost heap to cook like this for a few weeks, after which you need to mix it around with your garden fork (the stirring part). The best way to do this is to fork the whole thing into a new container, putting the top layers of your heap at the bottom of the new one. After a short while you will begin to find that creatures such as worms have moved in to give you a helping hand, eating decaying leaves at one end and turning out fertile soil from the other. Within three months your heap should have produced compost ready to use, sweet smelling and pleasant to touch. I always think decent compost should almost look good enough to eat in a bowl with a splash of milk!

Getting Started

You are about to set off on a fantastic journey that will reward you in many ways, physically, nutritionally and mentally. It is hard work, and it will take up a certain amount of your time, but you will experience self-gratification from your own physical toil that is not often achieved in our modern world. It has to be one of the best stress-busters around, as well as a good workout (no need for expensive gym subscriptions here!).

It always helps to have a few things sorted before you begin to dig, sow seeds or plant out your crops. I think over-planning can often take away the fun and spontaneity, but it's good to have a rough idea of what you want to grow, and how and where you want to grow it. My problem is that I get so excited I rush out and start digging like a mad thing, only to find the hose will not stretch to my newly dug patch!

First off, try to make your life as easy as possible – don't put your salad or herb patch right down at the bottom of the garden when you have space outside the kitchen door, in easy reach. Make sure that wherever you grow your plants they will have adequate sun and shelter, and a convenient water supply. Another tip is not to site your plot a million miles from your tools – there's nothing worse than having to keep walking to and fro when you forget the spade or fork. Again, you need to decide how much you want to grow – do you want to grow enough to swap with your friends and neighbours or freeze for consumption later? If you don't have much free time, or a lot of space, you may wish to be a bit more modest with your quantities. The trick is not to take on more than you can cope with, otherwise you are in danger of spreading yourself too thin – a situation that only leads to more work, and ultimately disappointing results. It's much better to start off small; you'll have more time to spend on your individual plants, which means you'll learn more and get much better results.

Once you have made some basic plans, it's time to get dirty! It is always best to start at a weekend, because this way you can fit in a day or two of good work and if you've forgotten anything you can pop out and get what you need without too much disruption. Starting a new project like this is always made easier if you have a friend helping, as you'll get more work done and have a bit of a laugh as well as sinking a few beers as you go!

The vegetable patch

Once upon a time most gardens had a vegetable patch filled with cabbages, potatoes and carrots. These are what I call grandad crops, because they were the vegetables my grandfather and his friends grew. I always think of him when I pass an allotment and see some fantastic old boy tending a beautifully cultivated plot full of crops like that. (I often wonder what these old gents do with so many cabbages – do they swap them for flat caps and braces?) If you have plenty of space, it's well worth growing as wide a variety of vegetables as possible, from the old favourites to the new and exciting. However, if your space is limited, you don't want to grow crops that will fill your plot up, take a long time to grow, or are readily available and cheap to buy locally. You are better off growing varieties that are fairly compact, and also ones that are early-cropping so that when they are finished they can be replaced by later-cropping varieties. The most important point to make is that you should only plant vegetables that you enjoy eating – if you don't like cabbage, don't grow them!

Salads

Salad crops have to be one of my favourite things. They grow quickly and can be on your plate almost as soon as they are picked. A further thing about salad crops is that the comparison between home-grown and supermarket-bought is so marked that they might as well be a different vegetable altogether. One great example of this is the iceberg lettuce, which has had much criticism over recent years for being tasteless and dated. I dare anyone to say a cross word against an iceberg once they have tasted a home-grown specimen with its firm, crunchy green leaves packed with flavour. This lettuce acquired its bad name due to the import of tasteless lettuces grown out of season, many of which have not even been grown in soil but in a nutrient-rich water solution. There is now a huge variety of salad crops to choose from: some you cut once, as large lettuces, others you just take a few leaves from, such as rocket or the cut-and-come-again varieties. The shapes and colours of the salads on offer are every bit as diverse as the varieties available, with yellows and reds, large flat leaves, curly leaves and some that have a feathery appearance. You can either buy small plants or grow your salads from seed – the latter is a much better way of doing it, as you can sow in succession to ensure a plentiful supply of leaves throughout the season.

Lettuces

There are many varieties of lettuce and they are all easy to grow, either as plug plants or from seed. Lettuce seeds are very small, which means you get plenty in a packet. Sow your seeds either in pots or straight into the ground from April to late July. Sow a new batch of seed every three weeks, to give you a supply of delicious lettuce throughout the season.

Cos: This lettuce has a fairly compact head, with coarse-textured, elongated leaves. It has a wonderful flavour, and when eaten young has a pleasant bitter quality.

Varieties include: Little Gem, Jessica and Pinokkio.

Iceberg or crisphead: One of my favourites, and, like the prawn cocktail, making a comeback from the eighties. This lettuce has a large, dense, green head bursting with crisp, almost white, folded leaves inside.

Varieties include: Webbs Wonderful.

Cut and come again or loose leaf: These are great lettuces, especially if you have a number of different varieties – you simply take the leaves you want for your salad, mixing and matching, without harvesting the whole plant.

Varieties include: Lollo Rossa and Salad Bowl.

Rocket

This peppery little plant has rocketed to stardom (sorry for the terrible pun) in recent years. It has become so popular that you really have to go out of your way if you want to avoid it – it appears on every restaurant menu, in numerous sandwich fillings and of course in bags of ready-made salad. It has become the iceberg lettuce of the decade. Its popularity is much deserved – the luscious leaves have a pungent, fiery quality that is almost addictive, and for me it has become an essential ingredient in many dishes both hot and cold throughout the summer. Rocket is really easy to grow from seed, and I sow it in any spare rough ground that gets plenty of sun – in fact, the sunnier the spot the stronger the flavour. Sow your seeds in spring and repeat the sowing throughout the season to give you plenty of young leaves. Rocket runs to seed very quickly – to slow it down, pick out the flowers as they appear. The great thing with rocket, as with cut-and-come-again lettuce, is that you can take what you want but leave the plant growing to produce more leaves. There are two types of rocket available: wild rocket, which has thin leaves with a concentrated peppery flavour, and the cultivated form, which lacks the wild rocket's intensity but has larger leaves.

Nasturtium

This plant not only provides a delicious addition to salads but also gives a dash of colour and beauty to the vegetable patch. It has a rambling habit and will spread far and wide, spilling over beds and paths and climbing over walls. Nasturtiums can be planted in any gaps between other crops and add a bit of informality. You can sow the seeds directly into the soil, but you should be prepared to lose a percentage of your seedlings to slugs and snails. To prevent this happening, sow your seeds in pots and transplant them when the plants are better established. Harvest nasturtiums by picking the young leaves and flowers to add to salads; the seeds may be eaten as well and are great added to curries or chutneys.

Spinach

Michaela, the love of my life, has to be the biggest fan of spinach I've ever met, even more so than Popeye the Sailor Man. The good news for me is that this green-leaved veggie doesn't really have the same effect on her as it does on Popeye, otherwise I think she would reach for a can every time I left the toilet seat up!

When the leaves are young and tender, spinach is fantastic added to salad. Pick it carefully so as not to upset the plant too much. When the leaves get larger and more fibrous they need to be cooked – simply wilt them in a pan with a sprinkle of water, then add plenty of black pepper and butter. Spinach can be easily grown from seed: sow the first batch in spring and continue at three-week intervals until early July to give a plentiful supply.

Watercress

This popular salad vegetable is now grown on a massive scale to keep up with demand for its delicious peppery taste. In the wild, as its name implies, watercress grows in and around the edges of running water such as streams. If you ever come across any patches of watercress growing wild around a river, make sure there are no sheep or other livestock around: if you eat it, you may be in danger of becoming a host to a liver fluke. Watercress plays an important part in the life cycle of this parasite – the fluke uses it as a way into its final host, remaining dormant on the leaves until it's eaten. I know this makes it hard not to be put off picking wild watercress, but it should give you more incentive to grow your own, and the good news is that you won't get a parasite and you don't need a river! As long as you can keep watercress well watered you can grow it as a conventional vegetable. You can grow it from seed sown directly into the soil, or if you buy a bag of watercress from a supermarket you can place a few shoots into damp potting compost or even a glass of water and they will soon root. Once you have your plants going you can harvest the leaves like rocket, pinching out the flowers as they appear to prevent it running to seed.

Greens

I used to hate greens as a kid – the word always conjured up images of overcooked cabbage or Brussels sprouts. Now I'm into greens in a big way; they are so tasty, and when you are eating them you just know they are doing you so much good. Greens are packed with vitamins and antioxidants; they provide roughage and are a great source of iron. They are fantastic cooked or eaten raw in a salad, and what's more they are now trendy. You have only to flick through one of the many glossy cookery magazines to find page after page dedicated to sprouting broccoli, baby leeks or seakale, and there is always a long queue at the vegetable growers' stalls at any good farmers' market. I try to grow as many greens as possible; they are easy to cultivate and for me a meal is not a meal without them. But despite my ravings I still cannot get into sprouts. It must be something deep-rooted in my childhood – having piles of overcooked sprouts heaped on my plate at Christmas and not being allowed to open my presents until I had eaten the lot!

Cabbage

Cabbages are generally seen as boring, which is a shame – they are far from it, and come in all shapes and sizes, as well as early, mid and late varieties. By mixing your varieties you will have a supply of greens throughout the year, which is very handy, especially in winter when most other crops have finished. Cabbages are easy to grow, but you will have a constant battle on your hands with the caterpillars of the cabbage white butterfly, which will soon discover your plants. The cabbage white will lay its eggs on all the members of the cabbage family (brassicas), which includes broccoli, cauliflower and Brussels sprouts. One way to stop these aerial attacks is to build a small frame over your crops and cover it with a fine mesh or a net curtain. This will stop adult butterflies making contact with your plants, but make sure you don't cut out too much sunlight. You can sow cabbage seed directly into the soil, or buy or grow your own plants.

Sprouting broccoli

If you want to gather fresh vegetables all year round, you should include sprouting broccoli on your list. This plant does not produce a large flowering head like the conventional broccoli we are all accustomed to, but lots of small heads on long shoots or spears. These small heads can be harvested along with the stem and cooked whole. They are amazing simply steamed and served with crushed black pepper, butter and a sprinkling of chilli salt.

Orach

This is a new vegetable to me, but one that has been around for a long time – it was commonly grown in the UK in the Middle Ages. It makes a very interesting alternative to spinach, as it comes not only in green, but also in a deep red. Sow the seeds straight into the ground around May, and when the plant is big enough, pick the leaves you need and cook them like spinach.

Kale

Another member of the brassica family, kale is descended from the wild cabbage and comes in a number of varieties, both straight-leaved and curly. As it is related to the wild cabbage it is extremely hardy, and many believe a frost improves the flavour of the crop. Kale is easy to grow from seed sown in early spring, and you should have leaves to harvest from Christmas onwards. To encourage more leaves to grow you should cut from the centre of the plant first, which will result in new side shoots. The picked leaves can be cooked like spinach or cabbage, and they're great added to soups.

Chard (aka seakale beet)

This is a beautiful and architectural vegetable, and very decorative when grown in a pot, especially the red-leaved variety. The plant gives you two vegetables in one: the stems can be eaten separately, steamed and served like asparagus, the leaves being cooked in a similar fashion to spinach. There is now a whole range of colour varieties, from pale yellow, to green, to deep purple, to red, and you can buy seeds in a multicoloured mixture. All need the same treatment: grow from seed sown directly into the soil in spring, to give a harvest in summer.

Peas and beans

Peas and beans are two of my favourite crops. They are both delicious and nutritious and are wonderful plants to grow, both for their architectural qualities and for their stunning flowers. Beans in particular are really fantastic, as they climb like monkeys; you can either build wigwams for them out of bamboo canes, or let your imagination run riot and create bean walkways or weird sculptures. Another reason I have such a fondness for these plants is that I remember seeing my dad growing them when I was small – I was always amazed at the way the seeds went into the pots and the green shoots developed into huge rambling plants as the weeks passed. Such experiences are extremely important for both child and adult: sowing seeds and watching the young plants develop give an insight into the miracles of nature, both spellbinding and exhilarating. There is something special that goes beyond satisfaction when you harvest fruits or vegetables from a mature, healthy plant that you've grown from a seed. It's the best way to get kids to eat their vegetables!

There are many varieties of peas and beans, and all are easy to grow. They come in a variety of colours, with the pods anything from green to white, dark purple or even multicoloured. The basic beans you should grow are runner beans, French beans and broad beans – the pods, picked when young and simply boiled, or chopped and added raw to salads, are delicious. The thing with beans and peas is to pick regularly, as this will encourage more flowers and result in more pods. If you want the beans themselves rather than the pods, you need to leave some of the pods to develop until you feel the seeds inside are large enough. These can be shelled and either eaten fresh or cooked, or dried and stored in airtight jars for use later. Mine never make it to the storage stage, or even as far as the kitchen, as I can't help eating them fresh from the pod while they're still on the plant! Beans, either cooked or raw, or even a mixture of both, make the best salads – all you need is a bit of garlic, salt, freshly ground black pepper, a dash of olive oil and plenty of chopped parsley.

Peas are grown in the same way as beans, and you should expect to harvest them around three weeks after they have flowered, while they are still young and tender. Fresh peas are like little bombs of flavour, and for me they were simply made to be eaten with rice, either hot or cold – amazing. Peas, like beans, have a climbing habit and need support – I usually cut branches from overgrown trees and stick them into the ground where my young peas are growing. This provides a good alternative to bamboo – it gives the young plants a more dynamic structure to climb over and the veggie plot a more natural feel. Peas and beans are easy to grow from seed, sown either directly into the soil or in pots in the greenhouse (or, as my dad used to, on the window ledge in the kitchen). Growing in pots indoors will give you the benefit of an earlier crop, but I also find that well-grown-on seedlings are more robust and often have a better chance of survival when they're planted out, probably because the farm is inhabited by so many animals that like to eat small seedlings as they appear, including one of my dogs, Bracken.

Roots, tubers and bulbs

This massive group of vegetables provides the staple diet for the majority of the world's population. Root crops consist of vegetables such as carrots, parsnips, Jerusalem artichokes, turnips and swedes. As the name implies, it is the root of the plant that is harvested – this is where all the starches and sugars produced by the plant from the energy of the sun are stored. Tubers, for example potatoes, are similar to root crops, but rather than putting all their resources into one large root, these plants store the foods they have gathered in tubers that act as mini-reservoirs. The more reserves the plant gains the more tubers it develops. What's more, each tuber also has the potential to become a new plant genetically identical to the original – not bad going for a potato really!

The final group of vegetables are those referred to as bulb crops. These are the leeks and onions. These plants store their food reserves not in their root system but in the base of the stem, which develops into a bulb similar to that of a daffodil or tulip. As the plant grows the bulb may swell to an enormous size – like those huge show onions. Again it is the plant's food store, in this case the bulb, that we are interested in. I am not going to go through the huge number of varieties available, there isn't room in the chapter and I haven't grown them all myself. However, I have picked one of each type – one tuber, one root, one bulb – that I find easy and enjoyable to grow.

Potatoes

There is nothing quite like the flavour of potatoes just dug from your own garden; it's such a simple, basic pleasure but it gives you a sense of belonging to the land that people often lack in their modern lives. If you have never grown vegetables before, you should have a go at a few spuds – they have to be one of the easiest crops to grow, and if you have rough soil they will help to break it up, making the planting of a different crop next year somewhat easier. Indeed, this year I have done just that: I planted, with the help of a few friends coaxed along with a number of bottles of cider, ten rows of potatoes to help condition a plot of land that next year will be planted with other crops. There are many varieties of potato and they come in a huge array of shapes and sizes, from early to late cropping. When buying potatoes to plant, you need seed potatoes rather than those which are for eating. If your seed potatoes have not begun to 'chit' (which simply means sending out roots), they should be placed on a warm window sill on a wire tray or in old egg-boxes until they do. Once you have two decent shoots on each potato, remove the smaller unwanted shoots and they will be ready for planting. Treat your seed potatoes as gently as a hen's egg so that you don't knock off the shoots; once you have them planted, you can expect to harvest your crop around four months later.

Carrots

Carrots are fantastically versatile in the kitchen: you can grate them to add to salads or coleslaw, make them into soup, mash them or just plainly boil them. But the main reason I love to grow carrots is for their juice, and I recently bought a snazzy juicer just for this purpose. I think carrot juice is absolutely awesome either on its own or mixed with vodka and ice, perfect while wandering round the veggie patch!

If you want to grow lovely long straight carrots you will need deep rich soil free from large stones. If a carrot root encounters a stone or a patch of hard ground as it grows deeper into the soil it will split into two or three sub-roots. This will not affect its flavour, and I actually like the look of misshapen carrots, but if you want long straight ones you will need the right conditions. If you are not lucky enough to have such conditions, you will need to create them, either by digging out long trenches that can be backfilled with loose rich soil and compost, or by building raised beds to which soil can be added to give depth. At the farm we have very stony ground that will never produce straight carrots, so as well as settling for split-rooted specimens I also grow short stumpy varieties that don't need deep soil. They are fairly quick-growing and are great in the kitchen, as all that's needed is to top and tail them before cooking. If like me you want to avoid unnecessary back-breaking work, it's well worth doing a little research to find plant varieties that will best suit your growing conditions – it will make life a lot easier in the long run. Carrots can be grown from seed sown directly into prepared beds and will need to be thinned out once they have germinated. A word of warning: at some stage you will undoubtedly have to lock horns with this vegetable's sworn enemy, the carrot root fly. The best way to avoid attack is to interplant your carrots with chrysanthemums – these popular bedding plants contain a chemical called pyrethrin, a natural insecticide. This, added to the plants' strong odour, will help to disguise the smell of your carrots and make it less likely for the carrot root fly to find your crop.

Salad onions

Salad onions or spring onions are full of flavour and add a real punch to salads, but they are also magic if you pan-fry them in butter with plenty of cracked black pepper, or chop them and add them to omelettes. Unlike most other onions, salad onions are grown in clumps – this restricts the development of the bulbs and gives them their characteristic shape. Sow your seeds in well-prepared soil that has been raked to produce what's called a fine tilth (it should resemble breadcrumbs). I sow my seeds from mid-March to July at four-week intervals, which gives me a constant supply throughout the summer. If you want to harvest these little chaps earlier, you will need to sow in September to give you a crop ready to pull the following spring. You can also sow in February, but this will require a little protection in the form of a cold frame or a cloche to get things going.

Fruiting vegetables

These plants are grown for their fruiting bodies rather than for the actual plant (e.g. lettuces), or part of the plant (e.g. potatoes). Fruiting vegetables include tomatoes, sweetcorn, pumpkins, cucumbers and courgettes. All are easy to grow, and among their ranks are some of the giants of the vegetable world, such as the massive marrow and pumpkin, which just seem to keep on growing.

Tomatoes

Of all the crops you grow it will be the taste of your own tomatoes that will really blow you away. You can sow seeds in spring in the greenhouse or in pots placed on a sunny window ledge indoors. Alternatively you can buy young plants well grown on and ready for planting out in early summer when the danger of frost has passed. Tomatoes like a sunny but sheltered position, and as they grow they will need the support of a garden cane. They are also very hungry and thirsty plants, so regular feeding and daily watering will be needed if you want plenty of delicious fruit. There are some fantastic varieties available, from the tiny cherry tomato to the large beefsteak type; some have a bushy growth while others have been specially developed to be grown in hanging baskets, ideal when space is at a premium. A ripe tomato should naturally come away from the stalk if you lift it slightly. Although green tomatoes are not very pleasant to eat raw, they make fantastic chutney.

Courgettes, marrows and pumpkins

These vegetables take up a lot of space on the veggie plot, although there are now many climbing varieties which will occupy vertical space if given adequate support. This allows these beautiful rambling plants to be grown in plots that would otherwise be too small to accommodate the conventional varieties. I always sow my courgette seeds in pots in early spring, either in the greenhouse or on a sunny window ledge, and plant them out into well-manured beds in May, when the young plants are well established. Young plants are at risk from slugs and rabbits, and judging by the damage to my plants this year I must have some very fat bunnies on the farm! When it comes to rabbits, the only way round the problem is to fence off your plot – it may mean a lot of initial work and expense, but it will save a lot of heartache and wasted effort in the long run. Once the young fruits begin to appear it pays to put a concrete slab or tile underneath them; this avoids contact with the soil and prevents rot and mould. The slab or tile will also act a bit like a radiator, absorbing the heat during the day and radiating it back on to the fruit, helping to speed up the ripening. The beauty of courgettes and marrows is that it is really up to you when you want to eat them. In Italy they pick them just as the young fruits appear, when they are still attached to the flowers. The whole thing is dipped in a light batter and fried, and is truly wonderful.

Sweetcorn

This is a very architectural plant and can easily grow to a height of five feet. This makes it fantastic for masking areas of the vegetable garden you want to hide, or for providing a windbreak for more vulnerable plants. Sweetcorn is in fact a member of the grass family, and unlike all the other fruiting vegetables described does not rely on insects to fertilize its flowers but on the wind. To get the best results from your sweetcorn you really need to grow them in blocks, as this makes pollination via the wind much more successful. These plants are not the easiest to grow, as they require plenty of sunshine and regular watering, but it's well worth the effort – fresh sweetcorn cut from the cob or barbecued whole is very hard to beat.

Soft fruit

Grapes

Grapes are one of my favourite soft fruits, and the fresh juice is a real summer reviver. I was always told that growing grapevines in the mild wet climate of the UK is a very specialized job, yielding little more than a few bitter fruits. I think in the past this was probably the result of growing varieties that either were not suited to our climate, or were wine varieties, or both. It is possible to produce a decent bunch of eating grapes in this country as long as you choose the right plant for the job and provide the conditions it needs. As a child my first experience of growing grapes was when my father planted four vines. Once established in the rich soil of our East Anglian garden they grew like wildfire. Although my dad's plants did very well and produced plenty of greenery, they also created a lot of pruning work. With a little research I soon discovered that we could reduce this hard work by planting

vines into the ground in large pots, as you would fig trees. Pot-bound vines have the added advantage of being able to be moved somewhere else the following year without too much disturbance.

I have planted two grape varieties, one red and one white, in our herb garden against a lovely old red brick wall – this not only provides shelter for the vines but also reflects the warmth of the sun's rays, which the developing fruits greatly appreciate. Vines like fairly well-drained soil and really benefit from a cold snap during the winter. When the colder months arrive they begin to drop their leaves, and once the plant has become dormant you can cut back the old growth ready for next year. I am desperate for a bumper crop this year – I want to try my hand at making my own raisins, which I have been told are amazing!

Strawberries

The smell of strawberries always sparks memories of family trips to our local 'pick-your-own' fruit farm. Once inside, my brother and I would set about shoving as many strawberries in our mouths as possible, while at the same time attempting to fill our blue cardboard baskets. After trying to eat our own body weight in strawberries, we had the task of desperately wiping our stained teeth and mouths before the weigh-in, quietly praying that our crime would go undetected. For me the hardest part was trying not to smile or laugh, revealing my pink teeth and tongue!

The only problem I find with growing strawberries is that I always plant too few, and once the first handful of ripe fruit has been eaten, often on the spot, I find myself checking the plant on a daily basis waiting for the next one. However, even worse than this is when you check the plant for the third time that day only to discover that someone else has got there first! The horror is almost too much to bear.

Strawberries can be bought as young plants and planted directly into your garden or container in full sun. Many people put a layer of straw around their plants, which increases the temperature around the fruit and speeds up the ripening, but also keeps the fruit clear of the soil where it might rot or be nibbled. There are many modern hybrids available that will produce good-sized sweet fruit, and most do very well grown in containers. If you get the chance, have a go at growing the wild strawberry, which produces tiny little round fruit that are pleasantly sweet. However, this plant tends to spread fairly rampantly.

Once your plants have fruited they can be cut back and left until next year, but you will need to replace your plants after two or three seasons if you want to keep yourself in fruit. You'll find that your plants produce lots of little baby plants which are put out on runners, and these will give you a ready supply of new plants for the following season. Simply pot up the little plants once they begin to put down roots and grow them on until needed – any left over will make excellent presents!

Blackcurrants

A real old English favourite, and a plant that the late great John Seymour called 'by far the most important fruit you can grow'. The little black berries burst with flavour and are packed with vitamin C. I love to add a sprinkling to a bowl of really good locally produced ice cream to add a blast of sharpness. Blackcurrants are easy to grow and long-lived, and will grow well in any part of the country. I've planted a bush this year but have also discovered some growing wild in my wood. They obviously do well in the dappled light, but also flourish in full sun; they will grow in any well-drained soil and really appreciate a well-manured plot. The best time to plant blackcurrants is autumn; however, I planted mine in summer because we were creating a new vegetable garden and it seems to be doing fine. A lot of people prune their bushes after planting, although this means you miss out on fruit in the first year, as the plant puts all its energy into stem growth. But it gives you a much bigger yield the following year. I didn't prune mine – it all depends on how desperate you are for your first blackcurrant!

The Herb Garden

Herbs are the essential ingredient in many dishes, and their fragrances spark memories of good times and holidays. Everyone should grow a few herbs – not having a garden is no excuse, as you can grow them in a window-box or even in pots beside the kitchen window.

Basil

I plant basil in the same container I grow my tomatoes in, as for me the two are as inseparable as Ant and Dec. You have to admit that there's nothing like a simple tomato and basil salad with a drizzle of quality olive oil – it makes you happy just thinking about it. (Funnily enough, basil used to be used to relieve depression.) The basil you buy in pots from the supermarket will last a short while on your kitchen window ledge, but if you put it in the garden the leaves will quickly turn brown in the sun and die. The best thing to do is to grow your own basil from seed, either under glass or in a sunny position indoors, or outside in small pots once the soil warms up. You'll be amazed how many plants you'll be able to produce from one packet of seeds, and how quickly they'll grow.

Chives

I think we should grow this herb for the flowers alone, which are perfectly edible and look amazing in salads. Chives belong to the onion family, and like all alliums they give a fantastic onion taste when chopped and added to boiled new potatoes or soups. I buy my chives as small plants, so they can be planted straight into the herb bed. The small bunches soon swell, and can be dug up and split to give you more plants – I love this type of gardening that doubles your money! Chives can be grown in most soils but they don't really like to be too dry.

Sage

Sage is grown both for its culinary uses and for its healing qualities. It is a plant that loves the sun, and in most areas it will grow into a stunning bushy plant around a foot and a half high, with beautiful flowers. Sage is the archetypal ingredient in stuffing, and whole sage leaves fried crisp are irresistible with a sprinkle of sea salt. The large-leaved varieties dry very well and can be stored for use when fresh supplies are at a premium. You can grow sage from seeds or buy small plants cheaply and plant them straight into the ground.

Thyme

This is another essential addition to any herb collection, be it in a garden flowerpot or a window-box. There are many varieties available, from small low-growing types to longer-stemmed varieties. You'll find thyme with green, variegated or even golden leaves, but at the moment I am addicted to lemon thyme, which makes great salad dressings. Thyme grows in most conditions, but to keep it looking nice and bushy and prevent it becoming too woody you must keep clipping it back every now and then. This keeps new leaves coming through. Any excess leaves that I cut and don't use fresh I tie in small bunches to dry or freeze for use in the winter months when the plant is dormant.

Mint

My experience of growing this herb hasn't been so much about encouraging its growth as about controlling it! It's a great plant for competing with many of the more invasive weeds, and I now plant mint in large pots which I bury in the herb beds to contain its ambitious intentions. If you have a fairly rambling garden and don't mind mint popping up here and there, why not set it free to do what it does best? The best and quickest use I've found for mint is to pick a young sprig, bruise it slightly, and add it to a long cool glass of gin and tonic . . . magic.

Parsley

A natural breath freshener, parsley will grow abundantly either from seed or as plug plants as long as it has plenty of rich soil and sunshine. I grow both flat-leaf and curly parsley for display on the butchery counters in our farm shop as well as to use in my cooking – both varieties are great stirred into sauces or freshly chopped and added to salad dressings.

Rosemary

You haven't got a herb patch until you've got a little bit of rosemary – it's a wonderful plant, full of aromatic oils. It is also a plant associated with memory, both in its use to increase one's memory and as a token of remembrance of loved ones. I have a couple of bushes in the garden that I raid, and I've also found a local supply growing around the car park of a certain supermarket which receives my attention on a regular basis. It always makes me laugh to think that inside they are selling sprigs of the same herb shipped in from various parts of the globe at great expense, when it is flourishing outside their front door for free!

Gardening without a garden

What options are open to those of you who yearn to grow some of your own food but don't have the space? Without going to the lengths of moving house, there are a few ways you can get your hands on some growing space.

If you are really serious and want to grab the bull by the horns, you could try your luck at renting an allotment from the local council. Such pieces of land are becoming rare, as many sites have made way for development, and once they're gone they're gone for ever. This is not only a crying shame, but is also theft, as more and more of our open and public spaces are being quietly stolen from our towns and cities – but that's another story for another time. If you want to go for it, and feel you have the time to look after an allotment, your first step should be to contact your local council, which ought to be able to help or put you in contact with a relevant association. Be aware that competition is often stiff, there may be a waiting list, and once you're in, you're in (don't worry, it's not the mafia!) and you will have a duty and commitment to that plot of land come rain or shine. It's like joining any organization in that you will be required to follow the rules – which in this case will mainly be about keeping your plot in good order for the duration of your contract. But in return for a very low annual rent (usually about the price of a small garden shed) you will have a plot of land where you will be able to produce a substantial amount of your own food – and you'll be keeping a great tradition alive!

The other option open to you if you want to grow vegetables and don't have a garden is to grow your plants in containers in any available space – on a balcony, a patio, a window ledge, even in some cases on the roof. For example, when I was studying for my PhD I used to grow all the plants for my experiments in a greenhouse on the top of a building in the middle of Coventry – it was my private little Eden in the midst of the urban jungle.

If you are growing plants in a container at any height the first thing you must be sure of is that it is secure and never in danger of falling and causing injury to any unwitting passer-by. You can use plant pots, grow-bags, hanging baskets, window-boxes, even an old bath tub – in fact, you name it, and with a little adaptation it can be used to grow plants in. How far you want to take things is up to you and your imagination, and to the number of containers you can get hold of! When using containers, don't just think horizontally – consider your vertical options. Ask yourself what can be grown up a wall or trellis, and think about using shelves to grow plants on – a kind of vegetable sky rise.

Pots

The fantastic thing about growing in pots is that you have a movable vegetable patch. It makes your plot a lot more flexible: you can move your plants to where they'll get the most sunlight or place them in cooler areas if they get too hot. Potted crops also have the advantage of growing off the ground, which keeps them out of reach of all but the most determined slug or snail. The one thing you have to watch when growing plants in containers is that they get enough water and food, as they can easily dry out.

Pots come in many different sizes and styles. At the very basic level you have your functional plastic plant pot used by garden centres and nurseries, while at the other end of the scale are your hand-made painted jobs, with elaborate designs. It's all to do with personal taste and how much cash you want to spend – I do like a nice pot but I don't see the sense of spending £80 on a pot to grow a tomato plant that has cost 90p! I use plastic pots to bring plants on, and then I plant them out into terracotta pots – I love the feel and look of terracotta, and it improves with age.

Hanging baskets

This is a good use of vertical space and these baskets are very versatile as they can be hung from trees, walls or anything that will support their weight. The key to hanging baskets, like pots, is regular feeding and watering. The bonus feature is that you can utilize a lot more space for your plants than you can with simple containers – plants can be stacked above each other and even grown through the sides of the baskets.

Window-boxes

A window-box can be a simple long trough-like container placed on your window ledge, or a more substantial creation fixed beneath the window on brackets. Again you will have to keep your plants regularly fed and watered if they are to thrive in this limited space. Window-boxes are great for growing rocket, cut-and-come-again varieties of salad, or mini herb gardens. There's something wonderful about being able to just pop your head out of the window, pick what you want and put it straight on to your plate without any fuss. You start to pick little and often, and only what you need. After a while you will wonder how you ever put up with all those little bags and packets of herbs and mixed salad that slowly rot in the fridge. Don't feel restricted by the number of windows you have available – long boxes can be fixed to any wall, and you could even build a number of them one above the other, creating a multi-level vegetable plot.

What to grow

Most of the vegetables, herbs and fruits described earlier will grow happily in containers, and you can now get varieties, both seeds and young plants, that are either dwarf forms or have been specially developed for container growing. To get you started, here are some of those I've had success with.

Salads: For containers you need salad plants that don't mind a few leaves being picked here and there, so choose rocket, Lollo Rossa and other cut-and-come-again varieties. You can buy young plug plants to put straight in, or grow from seed sown straight into the container. Once the seeds have germinated they may need thinning out, after which your lettuce leaves should be ready for picking within 40 days if conditions are favourable.

Tomatoes: Tomatoes do very well in pots and sunny window-boxes, and there are varieties that will be happy in hanging baskets. As long as you keep your plants well fed and watered you will get fantastic fruit – the restriction of a container on the plant's roots often results in a bigger crop of tomatoes.

Climbers: Plants such as peas and beans are great crops to grow in areas where horizontal space is at a premium, as these little scramblers will climb up almost everything if allowed to. If you have a large expanse of wall they can easily be trained to cover it with the help of garden wire attached to the brickwork. As the plants grow taller and taller their water demands will increase, so regular watering and feeding are vital for a healthy crop.

Peppers: I planted lots of peppers this year in specially designed containers – basically small black plastic bags with holes in for drainage. I grew my plants from seed, but you can buy young plants from the garden centre that are ready to go! Peppers love the sun but as a result dry out rapidly, so make sure you water them regularly.

Strawberries: Strawberries do well in containers, even in hanging baskets, and you can actually buy special pots that have been designed with the plant in mind. These are usually urn-shaped terracotta pots with a number of openings into which the strawberries are planted. Alternatively you can make your own with a simple length of wide plastic pipe placed upright with a series of holes drilled into it.

Herbs: Nearly all the herbs make fantastic pot plants, from bay trees to rosemary and thyme. I plant trios of different herbs in old terracotta pots outside the back door for immediate use in the kitchen. I love herbs – they are one of those rare things in life that combine practicality with beauty, since most, sage for example, will produce flowers that add colour to a drab concrete corner.

Potatoes: You can grow potatoes in most deep containers – I grow them in old polystyrene boxes, the kind used to transport fresh fish. Pot up two or three seed potatoes, depending on the size of your container, in rich compost. For a bigger crop, fill just half the container with soil to start with, and then, once the first green shoots appear, add more soil and another couple of seed potatoes. Keep doing this until the container is full. When the crop is ready I simply up-end the container and tip the lot on the floor – it sure beats having to dig your spuds up and amazes onlookers.

Gazpacho

It was on one of our family holidays to Spain that I first discovered gazpacho. When my dad found out it was cold soup, it was like watching that Peter Kay sketch about garlic bread! When it turned up at the table, however, he soon changed his tune and now he loves it. In fact when you think about it it makes perfect sense – what better starter on a hot summer's evening than a refreshing bowl of cold soup?

Serves 4

- 675g/1½ lb ripe tomatoes
- olive oil
- salt and freshly ground black pepper
- 225g/8oz fresh breadcrumbs
- 5 tablespoons olive oil
- 1 cucumber, peeled and chopped
- 2 green peppers, deseeded and chopped
- 2 large cloves of garlic, peeled
- 4 tablespoons red wine vinegar
- 565ml/1 pint water
- 1 tablespoon tomato purée

Preheat the oven to 160°C/300°F/gas mark 2. Put the tomatoes into a roasting tin, drizzle with olive oil and season with salt and pepper. Roast in the oven for about an hour, then remove and cool. When the tomatoes have cooled down, push them through a sieve or use a mouli to remove the skins and pips, leaving you with a lovely rich tomato purée.

Put the breadcrumbs into a liquidizer. Switch on the machine and slowly pour in the olive oil. Blend until all the oil has been absorbed by the bread. Add the sieved tomato and process until the mixture is smooth. Pour into a bowl.

Add the cucumber, green peppers and garlic to the liquidizer and blend to a purée. Add to the tomatoes in the bowl and stir in the vinegar, water and tomato purée. Season to taste, then cover and chill for at least an hour. Serve very cold, in shallow bowls with a couple of ice cubes added to each.

Garnish the soup if you like: chopped hard-boiled eggs, chopped spring onions, croutons and chopped cucumber are all good.

Carrot and Coriander Soup

This is a great soup: the carrots add richness and goodness while the coriander gives it a lovely fragrance and cleanness. This has now got to be one of the nation's favourite soups, and it's given the good old carrot a whole new lease of life.

Melt the butter in a large pan and add the onion and carrots. Cook gently for 10 to15 minutes, stirring frequently, but don't let them brown.

Add the stock and bring to the boil. Stir in the ground coriander and lemon juice, season to taste, then cover the pan and simmer for about 30 minutes or until the carrots are tender.

Blitz in a food processor or liquidizer, then return to the pan and heat gently, adding enough milk to make your desired consistency.

Serve piping hot, garnished with chopped coriander leaves.

Serves 4

- 50g/2oz butter
- 1 large onion, peeled and chopped
- 450g/1lb carrots, scrubbed and diced
- 900ml/1½ pints chicken stock
- 1 teaspoon ground coriander
- 2 tablespoons lemon juice
- salt and freshly ground black pepper
- 300ml/½ pint milk
- fresh chopped coriander leaves to garnish

Easy Peasy Pea and Mint Soup

This is a great summer soup – fast, fresh and very, very tasty. There's nothing like picking your own fresh peas, but frozen will do just as well here.

Serves 4

- olive oil
- 1 large onion, peeled and chopped finely
- 900g/2lb fresh peas, shelled weight, or frozen peas
- 1.4 litres/2½ pints vegetable stock
- a large handful of fresh mint, roughly chopped
- salt and freshly ground black pepper

Pour a good glug of oil into a large pan and fry the onions gently until soft but not coloured. Add the peas, stock and mint and simmer for about 10 minutes.

Season to taste, then remove from the heat. Cool slightly, then transfer it to a food processor or liquidizer – the soup can be blitzed until smooth or left quite chunky, or perhaps half and half, i.e. blend half the soup until very smooth but leave the other half whole.

Return to the pan and reheat, checking the seasoning.

Lavender and Honey Lamb

Serves 4

- 1kg/2lb 3oz lamb steaks
- sea salt and freshly ground black pepper
- 1 dessertspoon dried lavender
- 1 dessertspoon fresh rosemary leaves, coarsely chopped
- 1 clove of garlic, chopped finely
- 2 tablespoons olive oil
- 1½ tablespoons runny English honey

Lavender goes so well with lamb and honey, it's stunning. However, most of my friends look at me as if I'm off my head when I say I use lavender to cook with. If you are thinking the same, trust me – it's amazing. Lavender was widely used in cooking in medieval times, but you don't need to use much – it has a very strong flavour.

Place the steaks in a shallow dish and season with salt and freshly ground black pepper.

In a bowl, mix the lavender, rosemary, garlic, olive oil and honey together. Pour over the lamb steaks and use your hands to rub the mixture well into the meat. Cover with foil and leave for a few hours (preferably longer) for the meat to absorb all the flavours.

Preheat the oven to 220°C/425°F/gas mark 7. Put the steaks into a shallow roasting tray and cook for about 30 minutes, turning once halfway through.

Serve with new potatoes and fresh seasonal vegetables.

Potato and Leek Bake

I love dishes like this one: they are really warming as the nights begin to draw in and you feel winter is on its way.

Preheat the oven to 190°C/375°F/gas mark 5. In a buttered baking dish, place a layer of potatoes followed by a layer of leeks, seasoning in between. Repeat the layers, finishing with a layer of potatoes.

Pour over the milk and sprinkle with the nutmeg. Dot the top with butter. Cover with a lid or foil and bake in the preheated oven for an hour.

Uncover and cook for another 30 minutes, until most of the milk has been absorbed and the potatoes are golden brown.

Serves 4

- 450g/1lb potatoes, peeled and thinly sliced
- 225g/8oz leeks, washed and thinly sliced
- salt and freshly ground black pepper
- 300ml/ $\frac{1}{2}$ pint full cream milk
- $\frac{1}{4}$ teaspoon freshly grated nutmeg
- a knob of butter

Root Vegetable Crisps

This is another great way to get kids to try different vegetables. Whenever I have my friends' kids over I ask them if they like beetroot and the answer's always no. Then I watch them tuck into a bowl of beetroot crisps and it's great! Vegetable crisps are fantastic as a snack, or as a side dish served with game. I'm almost addicted to them.

You can make crisps with any root vegetable that takes your fancy, but carrots, parsnips, beetroot and celeriac are probably the best. Give them a good scrub but don't worry about peeling them, especially if they are home-grown or organic.

675g/1½ lb vegetables make enough for 6–8 people

Preheat a deep fat fryer to 190°C/375°F, or heat a large deep saucepan filled a third of the way up with vegetable oil.

Thinly slice the vegetables (keeping the beetroot separate), using a vegetable peeler, sharp knife or mandolin (watch your fingers!).

Working in batches, deep-fry the slices for 1 to 2 minutes until crisp. Drain on kitchen paper and season well.

Toss the crisps together carefully and serve at once or keep in an airtight container. Eat within 2 days.

Tomato and Onion Marrow

A marrow can be quite daunting – a huge green monster that makes most of us turn and flee! But don't be put off by its size, as it's full of flavour. Simply add a few tomatoes, onions and herbs from the garden, and the marrow will absorb all the lovely flavours. Excellent with grilled meat.

Serves 4

- 30g/1oz butter
- 2 medium onions, chopped
- 1 clove of garlic, crushed
- 1 medium marrow, peeled, deseeded and cubed
- 6 large tomatoes, skinned and chopped
- 2 tablespoons tomato purée
- 1 tablespoon lemon thyme
- 1 tablespoon chopped fresh parsley
- salt and freshly ground black pepper

Heat the butter in a large saucepan and fry the onions and garlic gently for about 5 minutes until softened. Add the marrow and cook for 5 minutes more.

Add all the remaining ingredients, apart from the salt and pepper, cover the pan and simmer for about 30 minutes or until the vegetables are tender. Season to taste and serve.

Cabbage with Onion and Bacon

I'd use Savoy cabbage or spring greens for this recipe, although any type of brassica would work well. Shredded Brussels sprouts take on a different dimension given this treatment too. For me this is proper food, no mucking about, just natural and full of honest goodness.

Serves 4

- 1 tablespoon olive oil
- 2 rashers of streaky bacon, chopped
- 1 onion, chopped
- 1 clove of garlic, crushed
- 450g/1lb cabbage or greens, shredded
- 150ml/¼ pint chicken stock
- salt and freshly ground black pepper

In a large pan, heat the oil and fry the bacon until crisp. Remove the bacon from the pan and set aside.

Add the onion and garlic to the pan and cook gently for about 5 minutes until browned. Add the greens and the stock and stir to mix. Simmer for about 5 minutes, or until the greens are just tender.

Strain the greens, saving the stock. Return the stock to the pan and boil rapidly until reduced to about 4 tablespoons. Return the greens and bacon to the pan and mix thoroughly. Season to taste.

Uncle Max's Chunky Pesto

Max is one of the local producers who attends our farmers' market. He tells us he learnt this recipe in Sardinia during his navy days, dating a beautiful Italian girl for the week he was there, and whose Nonna taught him to make this sauce. He says that, essentially, the secret is the basil, as it is too easy to use loads of oil and turn it into mush. This is his recipe.

About half the basil should be roughly chopped, discarding any tough stalks, into really coarse pieces, no smaller than 2cm/¾ inch in length, and put into a mixing bowl. Liquidize the rest with the olive oil and add to the mixing bowl. Give it a stir.

Toast the pine nuts lightly in a dry pan. Keep them moving and keep the heat low. Blackened pine nuts don't taste good and don't look good either. Add them to the bowl. Grate the Parmesan on the coarse side of the grater (the one you use for normal cheese), then add this to the bowl and give it another stir.

That's it – it will look quite thick, and if you are going to use it with pasta you might want to thin it with more olive oil. But it's best like this, with a chunk of bread and a glass of wine.

This makes quite a large quantity – enough for 8 helpings plus leftovers – but it will keep in the fridge for about a month if you ensure that it is always topped with a layer of olive oil.

- 200–250g fresh basil
- 450ml/¾ pint extra virgin olive oil (the cheap stuff makes it taste like magic markers)
- 70g/2½oz pine nuts
- 150g/5oz Parmesan cheese, coarsely grated

Mint Sauce

The ultimate accompaniment for any lamb roast, sweet, sour and sharp all in one little jar. True magic.

To keep

Wash the mint leaves and pat dry. Chop them finely and pack them into small jars. Boil the vinegar and sugar in a saucepan until the sugar has dissolved. Pour over the mint and stir well. Seal the jars and store in a dark cupboard. To use, dilute with water and lemon juice to taste.

To eat straight away

Pound the mint with the sugar in a pestle and mortar until completely crushed and well mixed. Stir in the lemon juice, vinegar and boiling water and leave to cool.

Makes 1 small Kilner jar

To keep

- 115g /4oz mint leaves
- 340ml/12fl oz cider vinegar
- 115g/4oz sugar

To eat straight away

- 4 tablespoons finely chopped mint leaves
- 1 teaspoon sugar
- 2 tablespoons lemon juice
- 1 tablespoon white wine vinegar
- 4 tablespoons boiling water

Herb Ice Cubes

A great way to add a little extra flavour and interest to summer drinks, as well as using up your excess herbs, is to make them into funky ice cubes. Herbs such as borage, most kinds of mint, lemon balm, lemon verbena are all suitable.

Pick the flowers and leaves of the plant and wash gently. Place one leaf or flower in each compartment of your ice cube tray. Fill with water and freeze.

Herbs for the Bath

Herbs added to bathwater can be soothing and healing or refreshing and stimulating, depending on how you are feeling.

The easiest way to enjoy herbs in the bath without having lots of bits and pieces floating around is to take a square of loose-weave cotton material such as muslin and place a good handful of your chosen herbs in the middle. Draw the four corners together and tie with a long piece of string. This herb bag can then be hung from the hot water tap so that the flow of hot water falls on the herbs as the bath is drawn.

Alternatively, long stems of lavender or rosemary can simply be tied in a bunch and hung over the taps.

The most popular herbs for the bath are lavender, thyme, linden-flower leaves and marigold. Chamomile is a soothing bath additive, while elder leaves or flowers provide a softening, healing skin cleanser.

Herb Teas

Herb teas can be refreshing, relaxing, restorative or just plain delicious! They are so easy to make, whether you use fresh or dried herbs. You can use a teapot, or one of those little mesh balls that hold tea leaves, or you can just infuse the herbs in a cup and pour through a strainer into another cup to drink.

The general rule of thumb is to use either 2–3 teaspoons of fresh leaves or 1 teaspoon of dried to each cup of boiling water. If the herbs are fresh, give them a rinse and a shake to make sure there are no little creatures hidden among the leaves. Pour over boiling water. Allow to steep for about 5 minutes (less for more delicate herbs like linden blossom), then strain and drink. Teas can be sweetened to taste with either honey or sugar, but for me the unadulterated taste of the herb hits the spot.

Rosemary Tea

Rosemary is reputed to relieve headaches. Just the aroma from the leaves steeped in hot water can be stress-reducing, so give it a go.

Mint Tea

Probably the most widely known herb tea and usually associated with Mediterranean and Middle Eastern cultures, mint tea is refreshing after a meal. Mint is also renowned as a cure for digestive problems.

Camomile Tea

Camomile tea is best made with the dried flowers of the plant. It's widely used as a calming and relaxing drink before bedtime.

Thyme Tea

Thyme can be quite a pungent herb, and a tisane of thyme has the reputation of soothing coughs and sinus-related ailments.

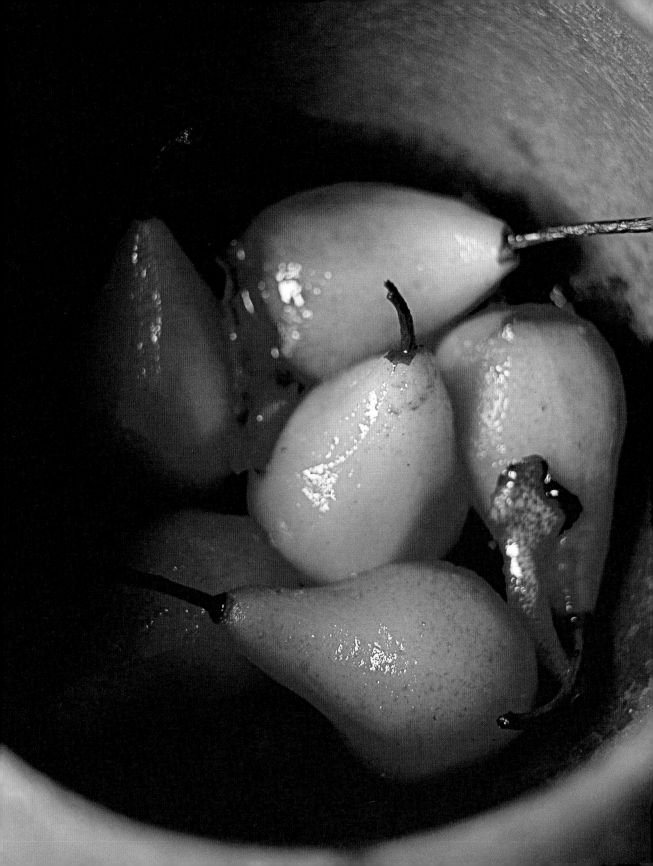

Pears Poached in Cider

Serves 6

- 6 hard dessert pears
- 115g/4oz sugar
- 300ml/½ pint sweet cider
- 300ml/½ pint water
- thinly pared rind of ½ a lemon

This dish captures the last rays of summer and welcomes in the autumn days. It is a killer dessert that's easy to prepare – make it in advance and bring it out when needed.

Preheat the oven to 160°C/300°F/gas mark 2.

Peel the pears, leaving the stalks intact. Stand them up in a large deep casserole and sprinkle the sugar over them.

Add the cider, water and lemon peel. Put the lid on the casserole and cook in the preheated oven for about 4 hours or until tender – they may take even longer.

Cool the pears in the liquid, then lift them out into a serving bowl. Pour the liquid into a small saucepan, removing the lemon peel, and boil rapidly until it reduces by half.

Pour the reduced liquid over the pears, leave to cool, then chill in the fridge until required. Serve with thick double cream.

in the garden

Lavender Biscuits

I first got into using lavender in cooking after a trip to Devon, where
I was served lavender potatoes, and I try to use it whenever I can.
Lavender biscuits are the ultimate companion for a really good cup
of coffee – the lavender gives the biscuits an amazing perfume that
makes them irresistible.

Makes 8 or 9

- 115g/4oz butter or margarine
- 115g/4oz sugar
- 1 egg
- 1 tablespoon dried lavender heads
- 150–225g/5–8oz self-raising flour

Preheat the oven to 170°C/325°F/gas mark 3.

Cream the butter with the sugar until fluffy, then add the egg and beat well. Add the lavender and mix in until evenly distributed. Add enough of the sieved flour to make a soft dough.

Place teaspoonfuls of the mixture on to a baking tray lined with silicon paper and bake in the preheated oven for 15 to 20 minutes.

Cherries in Brandy

Fruit infused in alcohol is simple but so effective. It not
only transforms cheap spirits into something to savour
in a glass after dinner, but also makes a fantastic simple
sauce to pour over ice cream for a boozy treat.

Cut the cherries in half and remove the stones. Put
the cherries, sugar, cinnamon stick, orange rind
and juice into a pan and cook, covered, over a low
heat for about 10 minutes. The cherries will start
to soften.

Add the redcurrant jelly and the brandy and stir
until the jelly melts.

Leave to cool, then chill until required. Lovely cold
with ice cream, and even better warmed up.

Serves 6

- 900g/2lb cherries
- 15g/½oz sugar
- 1 cinnamon stick
- finely grated rind of
  ½ an orange
- juice of 2 oranges
- 2 tablespoons redcurrant jelly
- 4 tablespoons brandy

Apple and Elderberry Pie

These two fruits make wicked partners in flavour and the contrasting colours are fantastic. I love the sharpness of the berries and the cooking apples with cream.

Serves 6

- 225g/8oz ripe elderberries, stalks removed, washed and drained
- 675g/1½lb cooking apples, peeled, quartered, cored and thickly sliced
- 30g/1oz plain flour
- 150g/5oz caster sugar
- beaten egg to glaze
- a little caster sugar

For the pastry

- 170g/6oz plain flour
- a large pinch of salt
- ½ teaspoon baking powder
- 85g/3oz unsalted butter, cut into small pieces
- 50g/2oz caster sugar
- 1 egg yolk, beaten
- 50ml/2fl oz double cream

Preheat the oven to 200°C/400°F/gas mark 6.

To make the pastry, sift the flour, salt and baking powder into a large bowl. Rub in the butter until the mixture looks like breadcrumbs, then add the sugar and stir. Mix the egg yolk with the cream and add to the mixture. Mix to a firm dough using first a knife then your hands. Wrap in clingfilm and chill in the fridge for 20 minutes before using.

Put the elderberries in a small pan over a low heat without any water. This will release some of the juices. Cook for about 5 minutes then strain off and reserve the juice. Mix the apples, flour, sugar and drained elderberries together in a bowl, then tip them on to a 24cm/9½ inch diameter pie plate.

On a lightly floured surface, roll out the chilled pastry to a 30cm/12 inch round and cut off a 1.3cm/½ inch strip from the edge. Brush the edge of the pie plate with water and press the strip on to it. Dampen the strip of pastry with more water and cover the pie with the pastry round, pressing the edges together to seal well. You can use a fork to do this or pinch the pastry with your finger and thumb. Use the pastry trimmings to re-roll and make decorations such as leaves or apples for the top of the pie. Brush a little beaten egg over the pie to glaze and arrange the decorations on top, making a small hole in the centre to let any steam escape. Glaze the pie with egg once more, and sprinkle with a little sugar.

Bake in the centre of the preheated oven for about 30 minutes, or until the pastry is crisp and golden. If it starts to brown too much, cover loosely with foil. The pie can be served warm or hot, with the reserved elderberry juice sweetened with sugar. And of course with cream!

Rhubarb and Strawberry Crumble

Rhubarb crumble is one of my mum's specialities and I have to say it takes some beating. But I may just have the lead with the addition of strawberries – the combination of the sharp bitter rhubarb with the sweet strawberries is incredible.

Serves 6

- 225g/8oz plain flour
- a pinch of salt
- 115g/4oz butter, cut into cubes
- 85g/3oz demerara sugar
- 600g/1lb 6oz rhubarb, washed and chopped into 3cm/1¼ inch lengths
- 2–3 tablespoons caster sugar
- 225g/8oz strawberries, halved, or quartered if large

Preheat the oven to 200°C/400°F/gas mark 6.

Put the flour into a large bowl with the salt and add the butter. Rub the butter into the flour until the mixture resembles breadcrumbs. You can do this in a food processor or with a mixer too – just stick in the flour, salt and butter and blitz briefly.

Mix in two-thirds of the demerara sugar thoroughly and set aside.

Put the washed rhubarb into a shallow ovenproof dish, sprinkle with the caster sugar and cover with foil. Cook in the preheated oven for about 15 minutes until starting to soften. Remove from the oven, stir and add the strawberries. Leave the oven on.

Spread the crumble mix over the top, and finish by sprinkling the rest of the demerara sugar over the crumble.

Put back into the oven for about 30 minutes (check after 20). If the crumble starts to get too brown on top, turn the oven down a little.

Serve warm with cream, ice cream or custard.

In the Kitchen

Everyone has an image of their perfect country kitchen, a cosy place with low ceilings criss-crossed by gnarly old beams, from which hang an assortment of pots and pans and bunches of dried herbs. One of the focal points of this nostalgic room is the large wooden table, beautifully worn though years of use, loaded with great mixing bowls and jams and preserves ready for storage in the larder. Such a kitchen wouldn't be complete without a cast-iron range, straight from the pages of a fairy story. On this cooking giant everything happens, from the ferocious boiling of the kettle to the lazy simmering of a stew. The other characteristic of the country kitchen is the wonderful heady smell that fills the air. The clean laundry drying, the bread baking in the oven, the washing-up on the draining board, the scent of freshly cut flowers, all these and more combine to give the kitchen its warm and familiar smell.

Some parts of this imaginary kitchen no longer exist, as they have been surpassed by technology, but the principles of wholesome food and the family live on in all good kitchens, no matter how small or urban. The old-fashioned country kitchen was the engine-room of the house, the powerhouse. It was a place of great industry – as well as the daily cooking there was also the daily laundry and washing; and it was a place where the family gathered and ate together, a rare thing these days. Most importantly, the country kitchen was where all the hard work of growing crops and rearing animals outside was turned into food and useful products inside. If the food was not cooked and eaten fresh it would need to be preserved in some way or another to spread the bounty of the productive seasons throughout the year. This was especially true in the days before fridges and freezers. This way summer fruits could be enjoyed in winter months, so you can see why it was important to make hay while the sun shone, otherwise

you went hungry when it didn't! Preserving food was done in various ways: either by making jam and conserves, pickling and drying, or cooking and bottling.

One of the most important areas in the kitchen was the larder, the store-cupboard where all the basic ingredients, such as salt, flour and dry foods, were kept. It was always well stocked, as there was no running down to the local supermarket to pick up a pack of this or a jar of instant whatever. The larder is still essential in any household that wants to achieve a little bit of the good life – it's like having your little store of magic from which a simple meal can be turned into a feast. At first it may seem more convenient just to go down to your local supermarket, but is it really? If you have a well-stocked larder all you have to do is go into the kitchen. I'm not saying you should stash loads of jars and tins like some neurotic squirrel, but a cupboard stocked with the basics, properly stored, soon becomes one of life's essentials.

Building Your Larder

Years ago the larder was where all the dried and stored food was kept. They were usually walk-in affairs situated in the corner of the kitchen, and were often built slightly below ground to keep the room nice and cool during the summer months. If you are lucky enough to live in a house that was built before or just after the Second World War you may still have one of those walk-in larders at the back of the kitchen. Anywhere that's cool, dark and dry will do as a larder, and modern kitchens are all now equipped with kitchen units and cupboards that do the same job.

Foods to stock

Mustard

There are so many types of mustard now, and if in doubt keep it simple. I always make sure I have a large pot of both Dijon and English mustard (for me you can't beat Colman's, but I would say that, coming from East Anglia). I also keep a jar of wholegrain mustard; it's less hot than conventional mustard but it has great flavour and is very versatile.

Table salt and sea salt

Sea salt, such as Maldon salt, produced less then twenty minutes away from where I live, is not only fantastic to cook with but is also useful for curing meat, especially bacon. Make sure your sea salt is unrefined and therefore free from any additional chemicals and further processing.

Honey

I always have jars of honey in the cupboard, mainly because I have ten beehives but also because I find so many uses for it in the kitchen. It's particularly good for making glazes. I keep both set and runny honey. English honey is among the best in the world, and eating honey that is locally produced is said to help prevent hay fever.

Pulses

Pulses are fantastic for stews and curries and have been a basic staple in many regions of the world for thousands of years. Store them dried, in airtight jars, and soak well before using, although lentils do not require soaking and need only a short cooking time. Pulses to have at hand are butter beans, split peas, chickpeas and lentils.

Oils

Oils are very versatile and can be used in salad dressings, for preserving, for adding to pans as a lubricant to stop food sticking. I always make sure I have the following in my larder: sunflower oil, herb and chilli oil (great for dressings), extra virgin olive oil and rapeseed oil, which is locally produced here in Suffolk and is amazing.

Sauces

Make sure you have soy sauce and Worcestershire sauce. Great for stir-fries and marinades.

Vinegar

You need red wine, white wine, balsamic and malt vinegar. Essential on chunky chips and in salad dressings.

Flour

You need self-raising and strong white flour. Flour is essential for baking but is also useful for thickening sauces and gravy.

Pepper

Keep supplies of both ground white and ground black pepper, as well as cracked black pepper and whole peppercorns.

Rice and pasta

You can now buy these staples in large bags that can be resealed, which is fantastic; alternatively once opened you can store them in large glass jars or Tupperware boxes with tight-fitting lids.

Herbs and spices

These give your dishes their characteristic flavour. You can buy herbs already dried, or you can cut them fresh, dry them yourself and store them in a jam jar. Spices are usually dried and are best kept in their packets – once opened, you can keep them sealed with a clothes peg. Here is a list of my essential spices: coriander seeds, juniper berries, nutmeg, vanilla, cloves, fennel seeds, chilli flakes, cinnamon, paprika and ginger.

Pots and pans

You don't need a flash set of pans to make fantastic food. The pan will not make your recipe tastier – as long as it does the job, that's more important than the style. However, it is well worth investing in a range of pans that are well made and will stand up to the rigours of time. The following is a list of the pans I use on a regular basis and quite frankly can't do without.

Frying pan

I have two large frying pans, one shallow and one high-sided, which allows me to both deep-fry and make things like pasta sauces. When buying a pan, test the handle to make sure it isn't too flimsy and that the pan itself isn't made from a thin metal material that can be easily bent or bowed under heat. As a student I went through loads of cheap pans until I realized I had probably spent a small fortune and had not much to show for it except for a carrier bag full of handles that had snapped off. It's well worth spending a bit of cash on a decent pan as it will save you money in the long run. My frying pans are decent non-stick ones that are just the right size to fit into my oven. Being able to put the pans in the oven gives you more flexibility when cooking – for example, you can finish a dish off under the grill or just keep it warm, which really helps when you are pushed for space. These two different sizes of frying pan cover me for a lot of my cooking needs, especially when they are fitted with lids.

Saucepan

As with frying pans, you should always test saucepan handles for sturdiness. A good pan should be well-balanced, easy to hold and have a snug-fitting lid. For basic cooking all you need is one small pan and one medium; a very large pan like the casserole is not essential but is very handy for dealing with large food items. There is nothing worse than having a bumper crop of apples or blackberries you want to cook and not

having a pan big enough to handle the job. Before I invested in a large pan I used to end up with the hob covered in an assortment of different pans filled to the brim while I hovered around them making sure they didn't boil over. I felt a bit like that guy who has to keep all those plates spinning on long sticks to stop them falling and smashing!

Roasting tray

A solid roasting tray is essential – make sure you buy one large enough to accommodate a large chicken and a few vegetables alongside. A roasting rack that will fit into the tray is also a good idea, as this allows the fat to drain and keeps the roast clear of the hot base of the tray.

Other essentials

- Grater
- Colander
- Lemon squeezer
- Measuring jug
- Kitchen scales
- Decent wooden chopping board

Kitchen knives

Six or seven knives will cover you for every kitchen eventuality, but most of you will be fine with just two or three. I can't stand serrated knives – they're cheap and nasty and quite frankly dangerous. A cut from a serrated knife is a messy one, and anyone who has received a nick will know how long it takes to heal. For me the only blade to choose is a conventional one with no frills.

To start you off, all you really need are a few basic knives. First a small paring knife for peeling fruit and vegetables and any other small detailed work. Next a chef's knife, which comes in different sizes from around 6 to 14 inches long. This is your workhorse, used for all general work – chopping, slicing, cutting – and will deal with anything from vegetables and herbs to cooked and uncooked meat. A bread knife and a carving knife are very handy, as is a boning knife because the upward tip of the point and the flexibility of the blade make manoeuvring around bones easy work.

When choosing a knife, hold it by the handle and feel its weight – it should feel heavy but comfortable, as well as being evenly balanced. If the blade and the handle are not formed from the same sheet of metal, make sure part of the blade runs through the length of the handle and is secured by at least two rivets. If the blade does not run through the handle the knife is poorly made, and after a lot of use the blade may be in danger of snapping off. Knives should be stored well out of the reach of children and in a place where they are easy to get out and put away. A dedicated knife drawer where the blades can be laid flat is ideal; a knife block or a magnetic strip fixed to the wall is an excellent alternative. Try not to store your knives in your cutlery drawer, as the blades will soon become blunt and it's easy it cut yourself while rummaging around.

A blunt knife is a useless knife. Sharpen your knife for a few seconds before and after use, to keep it razor sharp. A knife should be easy to use – a blunt knife requires more effort to cut through food and this makes it more dangerous because it's more likely to slip. There are a number of knife-sharpening gadgets on the market, but for me the best and easiest method is to use a steel. A sharpening steel looks a bit like a sword and is the method favoured in all butcheries and commercial kitchens. To sharpen your knife on a steel, draw one side of the blade, at an angle of about 20 degrees, down the length of the steel, starting with the base of the blade and ending with the tip by the time you reach the grip of the steel. This should be a smooth diagonal motion, and once you have done one side of the blade, carry out the same action on the other side, using the reverse side of the steel. Alternate the side you sharpen after each stroke, as this will help keep the sharpness of the blade even. Your steel should have some sort of guard at the base to protect your thumb and knuckle, but even so, take your time and don't be tempted to go too fast, otherwise you will be reaching for the plasters! Once you get the hang of the steel you will soon speed up, and a couple of strokes each time you use your knife will keep it in good working order.

Old Wives' Tales and Handy Hints

I love old wives' tales – far from being mumbo-jumbo they are wisdoms passed down from generation to generation, usually verbally and often in some sort of rhyme so that they are easily remembered. The keeper of the old country kitchen would have been well-versed in such tips and handy hints, which would have been vital to the day-to-day running of the house as well as making the most of whatever was available. I have a little notebook where I try to collect as many of these old wives' tales and handy hints as possible, because I feel that once this knowledge has disappeared it's gone for ever. I've listed some of those that work best for me in a number of categories; once you realize they actually work you'll soon find yourself passing on the knowledge.

In the kitchen

Keeping bread fresh

When I first heard this I thought it sounded like a load of old codswallop! But I have to say it really works. To keep your bread fresh, place half a potato in your bread bin. Michaela is mad on bread-making, but the problem is that, unlike industrialized bread, the homemade type goes stale very quickly. The old potato trick makes it last a few days more.

Fresh teapot

Once you have finished using your teapot, put a few teabags inside before you store it away. This keeps the pot dry and fresh, ready for your next brew.

Keeping your vegetables fresh

The worst thing you can do if you have bought vegetables in plastic bags is store them in the fridge still in the bag. Unwrap them, wipe away any excess moisture, and refrigerate them. If vegetables are kept in plastic bags they will begin to sweat, sprout and rot in no time. There's nothing worse than putting your hand in a bag to get your last carrots out and getting covered in a gooey slime instead.

Salt and pepper seasoning

A simple way to season food while you are cooking without using separate salt and pepper pots is to have a premix in one pot. Fill a salt shaker with both salt and pepper: for a balanced seasoning you want a mixture of three-quarters salt to one-quarter pepper.

Lemon juice

If you only need a little lemon juice here's a way to extract it without cutting up and wasting a whole lemon. Keeping the lemon whole, pierce it with a knitting needle or a small knife and squeeze out the amount you need.

Making the most of mince

When I was a student I always had my mates round for dinner, and although I would invite two, six would turn up, all expecting food. I found a great way to deal with this, especially if I was making spaghetti or a chilli, by making my minced meat go a lot further. Simply add a handful of good-quality medium oatmeal to your raw minced beef. The oats soak up all the goodness of the meat during cooking and bulk it up. My mates never knew the difference!

Tenderizing meat

Tough meat such as rabbit can be tenderized by boiling it in water with a little vinegar or wine for 5 to 10 minutes before cooking.

Too much fat

If you have too much fat floating on the surface of a batch of stock or stew, drop in a few ice cubes – the fat will solidify around them and can simply be scooped out.

Smooth gravy

Keep handy a jar of flour and cornflour mixed in equal parts. Put 3 or 4 teaspoons into a mug, add a little water, and mix well. Pour the contents into your gravy and stir well until it is smooth and thick.

Making a really rich stock

Before adding bones to a stock, try roasting them until golden. This will add to the stock's richness and flavour. Roasted bones can be frozen until you have enough to make a good amount of stock.

Getting rid of too much salt

If you have over-salted soup, stew or stock, add some slices of potato to absorb the salt. When they are cooked, remove them along with the excess salt.

Making food wrapping easier

I always get in a real mess with food wrapping and find myself with masses of clingfilm that eventually ends up in a huge ball, like dealing with a bag of eels. Keep your clingfilm in the fridge – the colder temperature makes it far easier to handle.

Peeling onions

If you suffer when peeling onions, try doing the job under water in the sink. This will stop most of the volatile juices reaching you. Alternatively I've been told that holding a piece of bread in your mouth helps.

Around the house

Smelly bins

If you have a bin that begins to smell, clean it out and add some salt – this should help stop the smell by creating an environment that bacteria do not like to live and multiply in.

Tight lids

To open a tight lid on a jar, use the handle of a spoon to lever the underneath of the lid until the vacuum is released. It will now open easily.

Salty boots

I spend a lot of time walking along the estuary, either fishing or collecting winkles and bunches of samphire, and if I'm not wearing my wellies the salt water takes its toll on my shoes or leather boots. Walking boots that have got covered in salt need to be washed in warm water and the leather rubbed with olive oil. Dry with screwed-up newspaper stuffed inside the boots. If they begin to smell, try sprinkling a little baking soda inside.

Lemon skins

When washing cotton tea towels, add the saved skins of a few lemons to the water – they will help clean them as well as giving them a lemony fresh smell. The best way to preserve your lemons after they have been squeezed is in a plastic bag in the freezer – just throw the skins into the wash still frozen.

Hangover tea

The older I get the less I can cope with hangovers. That extra glass of wine always seems such a good idea at the time, and you think to yourself that it really won't make that much difference! One way to combat the mistaken wisdom of the night before is a large cup of rosemary tea. It's a real pick-me-up: simply put a few young rosemary sprigs into a mug, fill with boiling water and leave a little while to cool before drinking.

Sleeplessness

The stresses of the farm influence how I sleep – there's nothing worse than worrying about a sow giving birth for keeping you awake all night. I find there's no point lying there wide awake – much better to get up, have a soothing drink, then return to bed. A cup of camomile tea really helps to send me back into the land of nod: infuse 2 tablespoons of camomile flowers in a pint of boiling water for 15 minutes, strain and sweeten with a little honey. Sweet dreams!

Cleaning

Removing stains from metal

If you have an old kitchen knife, a cutlery set, or even some old coins that have been heavily stained over the years, you can bring their original shine back with brown sauce. It works really well on copper – all you need is the cheapest brown sauce you can buy. Smother the items in the sauce and leave overnight – in the morning the majority of the stains will have been removed. Try it with an old two-pence piece – it will come out looking like it's just hot from the mint. However, it does put you off putting brown sauce on your bacon sarnie!

Cleaning glass

I've found lots of uses for vinegar other than cooking. Due to its high acidity, vinegar makes a first-class cleaning agent. Used on windows and rubbed down with scrunched-up newspaper it makes an excellent glass cleaner, just as good as those rows and rows of sprays you see in the supermarket.

Removing bird droppings

If you keep as many chickens as I do you eventually end up with their droppings in the most inconvenient places. And removing the stains can be a real pain in the backside. Bird droppings contain high levels of urea, which can stain woodwork and surfaces of garden furniture. Bird droppings can be a real problem if you live near an area where large numbers of birds, such as starlings, return to roost at night, especially when wild berries have been on their menu. To remove offending stains, rub in a little hot vinegar – this should help to dissolve and remove the mark, bringing your garden furniture back to new.

Cleaning a cast-iron frying pan

Before the invention of the modern non-stick pan, food was prevented from sticking to iron frying pans by the build-up of natural fats acting as a barrier. However, this causes problems when it comes to cleaning because soapy water removes this protective layer and as a result the pan rusts and loses its non-stick quality. To clean a cast-iron pan after use, pour in a little oil and a good handful of rock salt. Gently heat the pan and with a good handful of scrunched-up newspaper scrub the pan with a circular motion. The oil acts as a lubricant and the salt as an abrasive, removing any unwanted food. Once the pan is clean, rub it with a dry cloth and apply a little oil before storing away.

Cleaning dirty vases

A great way to clean up a dirty glass vase and give it a new lease of life is simply to give it a good scouring with hot water and crushed eggshells. It's very effective for removing large particles of dirt, as well as being an excellent way to recycle your eggshells.

Removing wax

Michaela loves candles around the place but I have a terrible habit of knocking them over, resulting in wax on the carpet or over me. I have found the best way to remove the majority of the wax is to lay a cloth or tea towel over the area and gently run a hot iron over the cloth a couple of times. The wax should melt on to the cloth, which can then be removed. Any remaining residue can be washed away with a little carpet shampoo.

Descaling the kettle

This is something my mum taught me, and it's a really simple but excellent way to descale your kettle without the use of those dubious and expensive chemicals that end up being poured down the plughole after use. All you need to do to descale your kettle is to pour in a good amount of malt vinegar and let it boil. Do this several times, after which you should thoroughly rinse the kettle before using it.

Cold tea polish

I must be the biggest tea drinker I know – I love the stuff! Tea has many properties, including a high tannin content, which makes it excellent for removing greasy stains, such as fingerprints, from varnished woodwork. Simply rub a little cold black tea on to a varnished wooden surface with a cloth, and polish with a duster.

Cleaning a burnt iron

When I was in the Territorial Army I was forever ironing my uniform – it had to be spot on for parade, otherwise you would seriously get it in the neck. In the end I became a bit of a pro with the iron; however, concentration often isn't my strongest point and I always managed to burn something or other, leaving scorch marks on the iron which would rub off on my immaculate shirts. One way to get rid of these marks is to let your iron cool and then give it a scrub with a cloth soaked in vinegar. After removing the stain, make sure you give the base of the iron a wipe with a clean cloth or you'll smell like a bag of chips.

Gifts, Decorating and Treats

There are many simple things you can do with produce you have grown in the garden or harvested from the wild that with a little imagination make fantastic and very personal gifts. A great thing to do at Christmas for friends and family is make up a hamper by putting together the odd pots of jam, chutney and jars of biscuits – you can't beat homemade produce, and it will far outdo anything you could buy in the shops.

Xmas holly

I always think those fake holly leaves used to decorate cakes at Christmas look so cheesy and tacky, especially when you can make the real thing for next to nothing. To make the classic frosted holly leaf decoration, all you need is a few freshly picked leaves. Wash them, dry them, dip them in melted margarine and cover them with sugar. Dry well in front of the fire for amazing frosted holly.

Herb pot-pourri

Dry small bunches of rosemary, sage, lemon thyme or marjoram and leaves of scented geraniums in the oven as described on page 289, or hang them upside down in the airing cupboard for a few days. Once they're dry, arrange them in a dish and add a little nutmeg for a real aromatic mixture.

Herb bags

The procedure is basically the same as for the herb pot-pourri above, but the dried herbs are placed in little muslin bags tied up with twine or ribbon. These bags are used to scent cupboards, clothes and drawers – try filling one with dried lavender and putting it under your pillow for a better night's sleep.

Pomanders

These were once thought to ward off infection and illness by releasing their fragrant scent into the room. The pomander is basically the old-fashioned version of those plug-in air fresheners, but with a more natural smell and far more attractive to look at. Pomanders are great to hang in a wardrobe or airing cupboard, filling the air with their perfume as well as helping to keep clothes moths away. All you need is an orange, some decent cloves and some ground cinnamon. Stick the cloves all over the orange until it looks like a rolled-up hedgehog, leaving a little gap between the cloves because the orange will shrink as it dries. You might need to make holes in the tough orange skin with a needle first, to allow you to push the cloves in. Roll the whole thing in a bowl of ground cinnamon and then tie a string around it and hang it up to dry for a couple of weeks before use.

Preserving

Preserving food has to be one of the most satisfying things you can do in your kitchen. It's a way of keeping your food for longer, capturing the flavours and magic that would otherwise be lost. Due to the convenience of the modern freezer and the fact that supermarkets can supply us with produce all year round despite it being out of season, the art of preserving looked in danger of dying out. Thanks to the Women's Institute and other equally dedicated individuals, not to mention an army of grandmothers spread all over the country, traditional methods of preserving food have lived on and are now in fact enjoying a trendy renaissance. The basic idea behind preserving is to be able to store food during periods of plenty, to supplement and add diversity to the diet during harder or less productive times. Preserving food is the best way to make use of your surplus crop, be it bought, grown or collected from the wild, before it is spoilt by time and natural decomposition. Decomposition is brought about by the uncontrolled growth of micro-organisms, enzyme activity, oxidation and dehydration (although in some cases dehydration can be a way to preserve food). How fast or slowly food decomposes depends on what it is and how it has been stored. As a result, the first rule to follow when preserving food is to begin with fresh ingredients. If the ingredients are fresh and in their prime, there's a whole range of ways of preserving that will retain their nutritional goodness. The food's original taste and texture will be altered whatever process is used, but the results will be delicious, will save you money and will be very useful. There are many ways of preserving foods and all are very simple and easily achievable in the most modest kitchen. I even managed it in a cramped caravan kitchen, so there is no excuse not to give at least one of the following a go.

Jams, jellies and marmalades

Making jams, jellies and marmalades is a fantastic way to preserve fruit, especially soft fruit. Although the methods differ slightly, the basics and equipment needed are generally the same.

Equipment

Kitchen scales

These are vital for weighing out your sugar, fruit and pulp or juice.

Long-handled wooden spoon

All hot fruit preserves need stirring to stop them sticking to the bottom of the pan and scorching, especially towards the end of the cooking time.

Large cooking pan

This is the most important bit of kit for making fruit preserves. Ideally the pan needs to be shallow and wide to allow good evaporation of the fruit, and big enough to hold around 2 or 3 litres, but the bigger the better, and I would even go for one that holds around 8 litres. This may seem very large, but it's important to have a big pan for jam-making so that the pan is never more than half full but still has room to make a decent amount of produce. The reason for this is safety. Making fruit preserves requires the boiling of large quantities of sugar, which spits and bubbles when hot and can boil up into a foamy mass alarmingly quickly without warning. Having a pan that little bit bigger gives you extra security.

Jam maker's thermometer

This not strictly essential, but it comes in very handy because it gives you the most accurate way of testing whether your preserve has reached setting point.

Plastic funnel

Vital for transferring your hot jam, jelly or marmalade into clean jars.

A fine sieve or jelly-bag

This is to separate any unwanted fruit from your preserve. If you can't get a jelly-bag you can improvise with a boiled cotton pillowcase or tea towel.

Clean jam jars

The jars need to be thoroughly clean and have a tight-fitting lid that will form an airtight seal.

Pectin

Pectin is something you will hear a lot about in the world of jam, jelly, and marmalade-making. It's a gooey substance vital in the process of fruit-preserving, and without it producing a preserve such as a pot of jam would be literally impossible. Pectin is found naturally in all fruit; so is acid, which also plays a major part in the process. During cooking the acid helps the pectin leach out of the fruit, then blends with the pectin to form a gel. So when you are considering making a preserve it makes sense to choose a fruit that is high both in pectin and in acid. Fruit that is slightly underripe has the highest levels of acid and pectin, and is the best to use. Fruit with low pectin levels can be encouraged to set by increasing the acid levels, which can be done by adding freshly squeezed lemon juice.

- **Fruits with high levels of pectin:** blackcurrants, redcurrants, green cooking apples, damsons, plums and gooseberries.

- **Fruits with medium levels of pectin:** raspberries, apricots, loganberries, greengages and early blackberries.

- **Fruits with low levels of pectin:** late blackberries, pears, cherries, strawberries and rhubarb.

Most jam is now industrially produced in large vats using concentrates, rather than whole fruit, often imported from various parts of the world. Once again, you only get out what you put in, and the resulting product is often an overly sweet chemically coloured paste with very little natural fruit flavour. Jam-making is a skill, an art form, it's like wine or olive oil production – you can't cut corners if you want the real McCoy!

In the UK we have a tradition of jam-making and we produce some of the best jams in the world. Just like the Italians are proud of their olive oil and the French are proud of their wine, I think we should be proud of our jam. For me a pot of jam is like a time capsule – it's a bubble of summer captured in a jar, packed with all those lovely aromas and vivid colours. It always brings a smile to my face to open a new pot of jam on a winter's morning – it's like letting a little bit of summer out every time you open it. Once you have tasted your own homemade jam, the cheap commercially produced rubbish that passes as jam in most supermarkets will never do again.

Strawberry Jam

My brother is a strawberry jam nutter. Every morning when we were kids, the jam pot looked as though it had been ravaged by a hungry bear! So this recipe is dedicated to my brother Danny's strawberry jam lust.

Remove the stalks and hulls of the strawberries and wipe the fruit with a clean cloth. Put the fruit into a preserving pan, or a large saucepan, with the lemon juice. (Strawberries are low in pectin and the lemon juice helps the jam to set.) Simmer over a low heat for about 15 minutes until the strawberries are soft and mushy.

Meanwhile, warm the sugar in an ovenproof bowl in a low oven. Take the pan with the strawberries off the heat and add the warmed sugar. Stir thoroughly to dissolve the sugar, then return the pan to the heat and boil for approximately 15 minutes. The jam should reach a set in this time.

Although a jam-making thermometer is not essential, it's useful for telling when setting point has been reached. The thermometer should be warmed in a jug of hot water before sticking it into the boiling jam. The setting point is 105°C/221°F, and the red line will shoot up to a degree or so under this to begin with. The last degree will creep up slowly. For accuracy, the temperature should be taken at the centre of the pan.

Makes approx. 3.6kg/8lb

- 2kg/4½lb ripe strawberries
- juice of 4 lemons
- 1.75kg/4lb granulated sugar

If you don't have a thermometer, you can do the saucer test: spoon a little drop of the boiling jam on to a clean, cold saucer. Blow on it to cool it a little, then push the surface with a clean fingertip. If it crinkles, a skin has formed on top and the jam will set.

Remove the pan from the heat as soon as you know setting point has been reached. Your jars should be ready, washed in hot soapy water, rinsed, dried and warmed in a low oven. Leave the jam to cool for about 20 minutes, then ladle into a jug and pour into the jars, preferably using a plastic funnel. Fill to within 5mm (¼ inch) of the rim.

Put waxed paper discs on the surface of the jam (these can be bought easily from cookshops and good kitchen departments in large stores), and seal with lids or cellophane covers held with elastic bands.

Very Easy Raspberry Jam

This is a classic jam, and I prefer it to strawberry. I love it with a chunk of Stilton and bread – which may sound weird, but give it a go.

Makes approx. 1.8kg/4lb

- 1kg/2lb 3oz ripe raspberries
- 1kg/2lb 3oz sugar
- 1 tablespoon brandy

Preheat the oven to 180°C/350°F/gas mark 4.

Put the raspberries and the sugar into two separate ovenproof bowls and put them into the oven for about 20 minutes or until very hot.

Tip the sugar into the raspberries and beat them together until the sugar has dissolved. Add the brandy. Pour into hot, sterilized jars and leave to cool.

Put waxed discs on top of the jars and finish with lids or cellophane covers and elastic bands.

Sweet Chilli Jam

You may have heard me talk about two crazy ladies called Jules and Sharpie who make fantastic chilli jam here in Suffolk. They started making a few pots in their kitchen, and selling them at the local farmers' market. Their product is so good that they now sell it in all the posh shops and to some of the most famous chefs. This is my version of chilli jam – I hope you approve, girls!

Put the garlic, ginger, chillies, tomatoes and bouillon into a food processor and blitz to a smooth purée. Transfer to a pan and add the vinegar and the sugar. Reduce the heat and simmer for about 30 minutes, until thick.

Pour into a warm, sterilized jar and allow to cool. If not using immediately, cover, seal and store in a cool place for up to 2 months. The jam will keep, once opened, for 2 weeks in the fridge.

Makes approx. 450g/1lb

- 2 cloves of garlic
- 5cm/2inches ginger, freshly grated
- 3 small red chillies, roughly chopped
- 225g/8oz tomatoes, skinned and chopped
- 1 teaspoon vegetable bouillon powder
- 50ml/2fl oz cider vinegar
- 150g/5oz soft brown sugar

Anytime Marmalade

I see marmalades as having two roles: the first as a fantastic breakfast preserve, and the second as a first-rate glaze for pork and ham – it really gives a lovely sticky caramelized quality. The most traditional marmalades are made with Seville oranges, which are available only in January. However, a citrus marmalade can be made any time of year.

Makes about 4.5kg/10lb

- 1.4kg/3lb mixed lemons, grapefruit and bitter oranges, whatever is available
- 2.8 litres/5 pints water
- 2.7 kg/6lb sugar

Scrub the fruit and cut in half. Squeeze out the juice and pips into a bowl. Cut the fruit into thin strips or, if you prefer, chunks. Put the peel, any soft pulp and the strained juice into a large, heavy-based pan and add the water. Tie the pips up in a piece of muslin and attach it to the handle of the pan with a long string so that it hangs well down into the water.

Cook gently for 2 hours until the peel is tender. Remove the pip bag, squeezing it with a spoon over the pan. Add the sugar and stir until it dissolves. Turn up the heat, bring the marmalade to the boil, and boil rapidly for about 15 minutes.

Test for a set by turning off the heat then carefully putting about 2 teaspoons of the marmalade on to a cold saucer. Allow it to cool then push your fingertip across the centre of the surface. If it wrinkles well, the setting point has been reached. If it only forms a thin skin or is runny, boil for 5 minutes more. Turn off the heat and test for a set again.

When setting point has been reached, remove any scum from the surface, stir well to distribute the peel evenly, and pot in sterilized jars.

Crab-apple Jelly

A jelly is basically the same as a jam except that the fruit pulp is drained through a sieve or jelly-bag to extract the juice. It is this juice, boiled with sugar, that forms the clear jelly. A pot of fruit jelly is a beautiful thing – held up to the sunlight it reveals its amazing vivid translucent colours, as good as any stained glass! Jellies are delicious eaten simply on toast, and they are equally good served with red meat, game or cheese. I love eating jams and jellies with savoury foods, and this crab apple jelly goes so well with pork. The sharpness of the crab apple really sets off the sweet flavour of the meat.

Wash and chop the crab apples. Put them into a preserving pan with just enough water to cover – about 1 litre/1¾ pints. Bring to the boil slowly, then reduce the heat and simmer for about an hour. Stir occasionally, breaking up the fruit to release the pectin.

After an hour, pour or ladle the fruit and juice into a scalded jelly-bag and allow the juice to drip through for several hours. Measure the strained juice and pour it back into a clean preserving pan. For each 565ml or 1 pint of juice add 450g or 1lb of sugar. Stir over a low heat until all the sugar has dissolved, then bring to the boil. Boil until setting point is reached – about 10 to 15 minutes (see page 275). When the jelly is ready, take the pan off heat, remove any scum from the surface, and quickly pour into small sterilized jars – this jelly sets very fast. Seal with waxed discs and finish with cellophane covers and elastic bands.

- 2kg/4½lb crab apples
- granulated or preserving sugar

Apple and Sage Jelly

For the best flavoured apple jellies, use a mixture of eating apples and cooking apples, and don't be scared of using windfalls. As kids we always used to eat the windfalls – we thought they tasted better but we also ate them because we couldn't reach the apples still on the branches. The amount of sugar required is determined by the quantity of juice yielded by the fruit, so have extra available just in case.

Chop the apples roughly, discarding any bruised bits – no need to peel or core. Put them into a large saucepan with enough cold water (about 1 litre/1¾ pints) to cover and simmer until the fruit is very soft. Strain the fruit and juice into a bowl through a scalded sieve or jelly-bag.

The amount of sugar you need to add depends on the quantity or weight of the juice. You can either add the same weight of sugar as the weight of the juice or, if you prefer slightly sweeter jelly, add 450g/1lb sugar to 565ml/1 pint of juice. Either way, pour the juice back into a clean pan and add the sugar. Bring to the boil and stir till the sugar dissolves. Boil rapidly for 10 minutes, then remove the pan from the heat and test for setting (see page 275).

Remove any scum from the surface and pour the jelly into small sterilized jars. Seal with waxed discs and finish with cellophane covers and elastic bands.

- 1.8kg/4lb mixed apples
- granulated or preserving sugar
- 4 tablespoons chopped fresh sage

in the kitchen

Bottling

Most of the preserved fruit we buy that isn't a jam or a jelly is in the form of canned fruit in its own syrup. This readily available produce has been the reason for the decline in the once common practice of bottling fruit. I think it's a great shame, as bottling is easy to do, uses up excess fruit and is far more pleasing on the eye than a can. Bottled fruit tastes fresher and truer to its original flavour than any other form of preserving, and in some cases the fruit's flavour is improved after it has spent some time in a light syrup – this is especially true for lusciously textured fruit such as pears. There is no real point in bottling small soft fruit, as these are best turned into jam. Larger fruit with a good level of acidity are better for bottling. The high levels of acidity are necessary to create an environment within the container which is unsuitable for the growth of bacteria, especially Clostridium botulinum, which would otherwise spoil the fruit.

Bottling is a straightforward process; however, it does require the proper preparation, the right kit, and planning. You need to set aside dedicated time, say a Sunday afternoon, to make sure you do a proper job – it isn't something you should do on the spur of the moment. Once you have been through the basics you will be trying to bottle everything! Don't worry if you overdo it – bottled fruit makes great presents. There are quite a few methods for bottling fruit, but I've chosen the quickest and one of the easiest, which is the water-bath process.

Equipment

The most important thing you will need is proper jars, strong glass ones able to withstand high temperatures and large enough to hold a reasonable amount of fruit. They must have lids that create a vacuum seal. You can buy purpose-made jars which are not all that expensive and will last for years. They come with either a clip fastening or a screw top. The rubber rings will need replacing each time you use them.

You will also need a thermometer and a large pan deep enough for the jars to stand in completely submerged, and which will accommodate a trivet in the bottom for the jars to stand on. Kitchen tongs are useful for lifting the jars out of the pan, and a wooden chopping board is ideal for standing the hot jars on.The jars should be sterilized before use. Soak the rubber rings in cold water for 10 minutes and dip them into boiling water before you use them.

Fruit and syrup

Almost any fruit can be bottled – it should be as perfect as possible and slightly underripe. It should be cleaned and any squashy or bruised bits should be cut away. Fruit can be bottled whole, although you can usually get more into a jar if you cut it up.

Fruits are bottled in sugar syrup – the quantity of sugar to water depends on the fruit being bottled. To make sugar syrup, put the sugar and water into a pan, heat gently until the sugar has dissolved, stirring occasionally, then boil for 1 minute.

Bottled Peaches

To make a 450g/1lb jar you will need 340g/12oz of prepared fruit and 225ml/8fl oz of sugar syrup to cover the fruit. To make the sugar syrup (see page 280), use 225g/8oz of sugar and 565ml/1 pint of water.

Clean and trim the peaches and remove the stones – if the fruit is halved it will pack down tighter.

Warm the jars and pack the peaches in, pushing them down with a wooden spoon. The jars should be filled to the top. Carefully fill the jar to the brim with the hot syrup (it should be 60°C/140°F). Give the jar a little shake to expel any air bubbles, and seal. If you are using a screw-top jar, screw the lid on tight but then unscrew a half-turn so that air can escape. Clip-fastening jars are designed to let steam out when fastened.

Place a trivet or rack in the pan and place the jars on it. Then completely fill the pan with warm water to cover the jars. Bring the water up to simmering point (88°C/190°F) over a period of 30 minutes, then continue to simmer at that temperature for a further 20 minutes.

Remove the jars from the pan, tighten the seals if necessary and leave to cool.

Pickling

Both fruit and vegetables can be pickled, but as with all forms of preserving your end product is only as good as the raw materials you start with. Your produce needs to be clean, fresh and firm – if you get this part right you are already halfway there. Large vegetables such as cauliflower should be cut up into smaller pieces, while smaller items such as pickling onions can be left whole and only need peeling. Fruits that are suited to pickling are apples, pears, peaches and damsons; small fruits tend to go mushy. Nuts such as walnuts can be pickled, and so can eggs: one of my favourite pub foods, pickled eggs are definitely something you either love or hate.

Pickles are so useful in the kitchen: they turn the leftovers from the night-before's roast into a feast, and a few sharp pickled onions, a slice of brown bread and a hunk of cheese has to be one of life's simple pleasures. Compared to the other methods of preserving so far described, pickling is relatively free from failure and pitfalls. I find it a relaxing pastime, pottering around the kitchen on one of those golden autumn afternoons, the ultimate stress-buster – forget pilates or yoga!

Sweet Pickled Peppers

This is a great way to store excess home-grown peppers. You can serve them with olives and slices of salami with drinks, or use them as a stand-by to liven up pasta and other dishes.

Cut each pepper into quarters lengthwise, removing the stalk and the seeds. Lay them on a grill pan, skin side up, and grill until the skin is black – you'll probably have to do this in batches.

Remove them from the grill pan while they're still hot, put them into a bowl and cover them with clingfilm. The steam will loosen the skins. Leave until cool.

While the peppers are cooling, make the spiced vinegar. In a pan gently heat the salt, sugar, sherry and vinegar to a simmer and stir until the salt and sugar have dissolved. Leave to cool.

Remove the skins from the peppers. Pack the peppers into jars and cover with the spiced vinegar.

Makes approx 1.8kg/4lb

- 6 each of red, green and yellow peppers
- 1 teaspoon salt
- 50g/2oz sugar
- a small glass of sherry
- 565ml/1 pint white vinegar

Pickled Onions

I got into pickled onions at a very early age, mainly because my dad is a pickled onion freak. He would quite happily sit and eat a whole jarful, with a chunk of Cheddar. I've got to say I'm not far behind him, and the sharper the better!

Makes approx. 2kg/4 ½ lb

- 1.8kg/4lb pickling onions
- 50g/2oz white peppercorns
- 30g/1oz allspice berries
- 6 cloves
- 2.3 litres/4 pints distilled malt vinegar
- 1½ level tablespoons salt

Put the onions into a large bowl and pour boiling water over them. Drain, then plunge them into cold water. This makes the onions easier to peel.

Peel the onions and set aside in a bowl.

Tie the peppercorns, allspice and cloves in a square piece of muslin and put into a large saucepan with the vinegar and salt. Bring to the boil and simmer for 3 minutes, skimming off any scum that appears. Discard the spices.

Add the onions and simmer for a couple of minutes until they start to look transparent.

Strain off the hot vinegar from the onions and reserve. Pack the onions tightly into clean, warm jars and pour in enough hot vinegar to cover them completely. When cold, screw the lids on the jars and store in a cool place for at least 1 month before eating. Use within 6 months.

Spiced Green Beans

The only problem with growing your own vegetables is that all of a sudden you are faced with a massive glut of produce, and this is especially true of green beans. This is a great recipe to preserve your beans so that you will be enjoying them all through the winter, well after they have been harvested.

Bring the cold water and salt to the boil in a large pan. Add the beans and simmer for 5 to 8 minutes until just tender. Drain and put to one side.

Put the pickling spice with the lemon rind in a small square of muslin and tie into a little bundle. Put all the remaining ingredients into a pan, add the muslin bundle and boil for 5 minutes. Reduce the heat, add the beans to the pan and simmer for 5 minutes.

Strain the beans, reserving the liquid and removing the muslin bag, and pack them into large, sterilized jars – they look cool if you pack them vertically. Pour over the vinegar and seal.

Makes approx. 700g/1½ lb

- 300ml/½ pint cold water
- 1½ teaspoons salt
- 450g/1lb small French beans, trimmed
- 1 tablespoon pickling spice
- 4 strips of lemon rind
- 30g/1oz sugar
- 450ml/¾ pint cider vinegar
- 150ml/¼ pint hot water

Drying

Drying food has to be the oldest and simplest of all the preserving methods. The practice of drying has been around for thousands of years, ever since early man discovered that fruit laid out in the hot sun soon became desiccated and could be stored for leaner times. The great thing about dried foods is that they take up very little space and can be easily put away to use later or eaten just as they are for a quick snack. Drying preserves food by depriving bacteria, which would otherwise spoil the food, of one of their vital resources – water. The lower the moisture content, the harder it is for bacteria to survive. In the UK we can't really rely on long periods of sunshine to dry food effectively. If the weather is really good it's achievable, although every time I try to dry a glut of fruit in the sunshine it always coincides with that time of year when there are plagues of hungry wasps ready to take advantage of any available food resource. As the British climate is variable, the best way to dry food is in your oven. There are now a number of specialized food driers on the market, which are very effective and worth the investment if you are going to dry food regularly on a large scale. If the oven is not an option, a rack set up in an airing cupboard or over a boiler will have the same effect, though the drying process will take a number of days as opposed to a few hours. In theory you can dry anything, but I'm going to concentrate on fruit, mushrooms and herbs to get you started as they are fairly straightforward and will give good results. Once you have mastered these basic foods you will soon want to experiment with all sorts of produce.

Drying fruit using the oven

The drying time will depend on the fruit you are using. Some fruit can be dried whole, while others will need to be either cut in half or sliced. Put your fruit on a metal rack and dry in the oven at 50°C/120°F for the first hour. After this, turn the temperature up to 65°C/150°F and dry the fruit for a further 3 to 6 hours depending on size and type. If the temperature is higher than 50°C to start with, the skin of the fruit will harden too quickly and burst. The finished product should feel springy and soft but not brittle. To test if your fruit is dried properly give it a little squeeze; if any moisture comes out it will need further drying in the oven. Once dried, cover the fruit with a dry tea towel and leave it to cool. Dried fruit doesn't have to be stored in airtight containers but it must be kept in an area that is free of damp.

Drying apricots, peaches and plums

Fruits with large stones can shrink during drying, so make sure you choose large ripe fruit that are firm. Cut the fruit in half, remove the stone, and place them on a rack with the skin side facing down so that the juice doesn't drip. Dry the halved fruit slowly at 50°C/120°F until the skin shrivels, then turn the oven up to 65°C/150°F, keeping the oven door ajar to allow moisture to escape. The fruit is ready when you can squeeze it without any juice coming out; the skin should remain unbroken.

Drying apples

Peel and core your apple and cut it crossways into slices, making lovely apple rings with a hole in the centre. Once an apple has had a bite taken out of it or has been cut open it goes brown very quickly, so to stop this happening to your rings drop them into a bowl of salty water (1 teaspoon to every 1 litre/1¾ pints) before drying. Cut lengths of bamboo garden cane to fit on to the grooves where the shelves normally go in your oven, and soak them in water to prevent them burning. After their salty bath, dry your apple segments and thread them on to the canes. Remove the shelves and rest the canes in the grooves. Heat the oven to 50°C/120°F, turn it up to 65°C/150°F after the first hour, and leave the oven door slightly open during the drying time. Drying should take 4 or 5 hours. Leave the apple rings to cool overnight on their canes, either still in the oven or suspended between two mugs.

Drying pears

Follow the instructions for apples but instead of cutting the pears into slices cut them into quarters. Give them the salt-water-bath treatment to prevent browning, and place them on a wire rack rather than on canes.

Drying mushrooms

All mushrooms can be dried and rehydrated at a later date when required, but field mushrooms are one of the best. Remove the stalks from the mushrooms, trim off any ragged edges, and remove any dirt or loose material with a damp cloth. Use a large needle to thread the mushrooms on to a long length of butcher's string, tying a knot after each mushroom to stop it slipping. The mushrooms need to be spaced along the string so they are not touching each other, otherwise they will not dry properly. You can either dry them in the oven by removing all the shelves but the top one, from which you can hang the string, or you can hang them up for a few days in an airing cupboard. Once the mushrooms are dried you can store them in a container or hang them up in the kitchen.

Drying herbs

Fresh herbs are not always available all year round in this country, and if you grow your own it is worth preserving them by drying. The two most important elements when you are drying herbs at home are temperature, which should be between 50°C/120°F and 65°C/150°F, and plenty of air movement – if the drying temperature is too high the herbs will shrivel up. You can dry your herbs over a period of time by tying them into large bunches and hanging them upside down in an airing cupboard, warm attic or garage, or you can dry them much more quickly on a sheet of foil in the oven for a few hours on the lowest setting. Once the herbs are dry you can leave them in their bunches and hang them in your kitchen, which suits herbs such as rosemary – it gives a rustic look and makes the house smell amazing – or you can strip the leaves from the stalks and store them in jam jars, which works very well for herbs with small or fine leaves. As well as the leaves, you can dry the seeds of herbs such as fennel and coriander. The best time to pick herbs for drying is when the flowers are still in bud, as this is when their aromatic oils are at their most pungent.

Tomato Chutney

Tomatoes make a mean chutney, and this is a recipe that really makes the most of these fantastic fruits. Use home-grown if you've got them – if not, buy decent toms from a trusted greengrocer or farmers' market. I don't see any point in preserving those tasteless tomatoes you can buy year round in the supermarket!

Put all the ingredients into a large saucepan and simmer for about 2 hours. Leave to cool a little.

Pour into clean, sterilized jars and seal when cold. Watch out for the cloves when you are eating it – they will need to be removed!

Makes about 6 jars

- 1.8kg/4lb tomatoes, skinned and deseeded
- 225g/8oz sultanas
- 340g/12oz apples, peeled, cored and diced
- 1 tablespoon salt
- 15g/$\frac{1}{2}$oz ground ginger
- 15g/$\frac{1}{2}$oz cloves, slightly crushed
- $\frac{1}{2}$ teaspoon mustard seeds, slightly crushed
- 30g/1oz fresh chillies, deseeded and shredded
- 2 large cloves of garlic, peeled and crushed
- 2 onions, finely chopped
- 115g/4oz sugar
- 565ml/1 pint vinegar

Caela's Cheesy Chilli Sticks

This is Michaela's version of the cheesy stick party classic, but you may notice a spicy difference! Apart from tasting fantastic, there's another very good reason for this. The chilli is a relic from Michaela's childhood. Her father, Michael, was an officer serving in the prestigious 7th Gurkha Rifles. This meant long postings to Nepal, recruiting the tough young men of the local hill tribes who make the Gurkhas among the best fighting forces in the world. While Michael was busy putting the volunteers through the rigorous selection process, Michaela and her siblings were growing up immersed in Nepalese culture. Her early upbringing is the reason why she loves spicy foods and why chilli tends to creep in wherever possible. The chilli really has a bite – perhaps there is a little bit of Gurkha hiding in every one of them.

Makes about 24

- 115g/4oz butter, softened
- 225g/8oz plain flour
- ¼ teaspoon salt
- 115g/4oz Cheddar cheese, grated
- 1 egg yolk
- finely grated Parmesan cheese
- chilli powder

Preheat the oven to 230°C/450°F/gas mark 8.

Rub the butter, flour and salt together until the mixture resembles breadcrumbs. Mix in the Cheddar cheese and egg yolk to form a soft dough.

Roll out on a floured board to a rectangle 18 x 25cm (7 x 10 inches).

Sprinkle over the Parmesan cheese and chilli powder to taste and cut into approximately 24 fingers. Transfer to a lightly greased baking sheet and cook for 8 to 10 minutes until golden. Leave to cool on a rack before serving.

Gingerbread Pigs

It's obvious why I make pigs, but don't feel you have to – make any shape you like. This recipe reminds me of my school days, when me and a few mates would sneak off to the baker in the village at lunchtime to buy gingerbread men. We would walk back to school munching away, that lovely crunch followed by the sweet and spicy flavour. Well worth the detention!

Makes 8–12

- 115g/4oz butter
- 115g/4oz caster sugar
- 1 tablespoon warmed golden syrup
- 225g/8oz plain flour
- $\frac{1}{4}$ teaspoon bicarbonate of soda
- 1 teaspoon ground ginger

Preheat the oven to 200°C/400°F/gas mark 6.

Cream the butter and sugar together until light and fluffy. Add the syrup, flour, bicarbonate of soda and ginger and mix to form a firm dough.

Roll out on a lightly floured board and cut out shapes with a cookie cutter.

Bake in the preheated oven for approximately 10 minutes, until golden brown. Cool slightly, then transfer to a cooling rack.

Muffins

According to my nan, when muffins were at the height of their popularity in the early 1900s each town had its Muffin Man, who used to walk the streets with a tray of muffins on his head. I'm not suggesting you should do the same, but a muffin, carefully torn apart while still warm, spread thickly with butter and eaten immediately, is a taste experience must.

If using fresh yeast, dissolve it in the warm milk. If you have dried yeast, sprinkle it over the milk and leave in a warm place until it is frothy – it takes about 15 minutes.

Sift the flour and salt into a large bowl. Make a well in the middle and pour the yeast mixture into it. Mix in the flour until it forms a smooth dough. Turn the dough out on to a floured surface and knead for about 10 minutes until smooth, silky and elastic. Place in a clean bowl, cover with a clean tea towel and leave in a warm place for about an hour to rise. It should double in size.

Roll out the dough on a floured surface until about 1cm/½ inch thick, then cover with the tea towel and leave to rest for 5 minutes. Cut into rounds with a plain cookie cutter – 7.5cm/3 inches is a good size. Place on a well-floured baking tray and dust the tops with the semolina and flour mixture. Cover with the tea towel and leave to rise until doubled in size.

Lightly oil a griddle or heavy-based frying pan and heat over a moderate heat. Cook the muffins for 5 to 6 minutes, then turn them over and cook for a further 6 to 7 minutes.

Makes 12

- 15g/½oz fresh yeast or 7g/¼oz dried
- 300ml/½ pint warm milk
- 450g/1lb strong white flour
- 1 teaspoon salt
- 1 teaspoon plain flour and 1 teaspoon semolina, mixed together, for dusting

Suffolk Cakes

I love any recipe that celebrates a region – it makes our country's food culture so much richer, and the people of that particular region proud of their area's specialities. As I live in Suffolk I was determined to add as many local recipes as possible, and here is a great one that dates back nearly 150 years!

Makes 14

- 115g/4oz butter
- 4 eggs
- 225g/8oz caster sugar
- grated zest of ½ a lemon
- 150g/4oz self-raising flour

Preheat the oven to 200°C/400°F/gas mark 6.

Warm the butter until it has melted but not coloured. Leave to cool.

Separate the eggs into two bowls. Beat the yolks together. Whisk the whites until they are floppy and just hold a peak. Fold the yolks, sugar and grated lemon zest into the whites. Beat in the melted butter, and stir in the flour.

Beat the mixture well and pour into greased bun tins. Bake in the preheated oven for 10 to 15 minutes.

Tea Bread

My stockman's wife, Sue, must make the best tea breads in the world, but like any good cook she will not give up her secrets that easily. So here is my version of Sue's classic tea bread.

Preheat the oven to 170°C/325°F/gas mark 3.

Put the tea, butter, sugar and fruit into a saucepan over a low heat and simmer for about 15 minutes until the fruit is plump. Leave to cool, then beat in the flour, spices and eggs.

Put the mixture into a greased and lined 20cm/8 inch diameter cake tin and bake in the preheated oven for 2 hours, until cooked through. Leave to cool.

Serve with or without butter.

Serves 6–8

- 1 cup of black tea
- 170g/6oz butter
- 225g/8oz soft brown sugar
- 340g/12oz mixed dried fruit
- 340g/12oz self-raising flour
- 1 teaspoon ground mixed spice
- 1 teaspoon ground cinnamon
- 3 eggs, beaten

Lemon Curd

I love breakfast times, getting all the preserves out and spreading them over hot toast. One of the best has to be lemon curd, especially the homemade version. This recipe has a real citrus zing.

Wash and dry the lemons. Finely grate the rind only (not the pith). Squeeze the juice into a heavy saucepan and add the butter, sugar and lemon rind. Add the eggs and heat very gently, stirring all the time, until the mixture is thick.

Strain into another pan, then ladle into sterilized jars. Keep refrigerated once opened and eat within a week.

Makes about 450g/1lb

- 2 large lemons
- 85g/3oz butter
- 225g/8oz sugar
- 3 eggs, lightly beaten

Aunt Thelma's Easiest Sticky Toffee Pudding

Aunty Thelma is my mate Nikki's aunt and I first met her on a boat on the Thames. She's a wonderful lady with a broad Halifax accent, and makes a mean sticky toffee pudding. Sheer indulgence!

Serves 6

- 170g/6oz stoned dates, roughly chopped
- 285ml/½ pint boiling water
- 50g/2oz softened butter
- 170g/6oz granulated sugar
- 225g/8oz plain flour
- 1 teaspoon baking powder
- 1 egg
- 1 teaspoon bicarbonate of soda
- 1 teaspoon vanilla essence

For the toffee sauce

- 85g/3oz butter
- 150g/5oz dark muscovado sugar
- 6 tablespoons double cream

Preheat the oven to 180°C/350°F/gas mark 4.

Soak the dates in the boiling water and set aside. Cream the butter and the sugar together. Sift the flour and the baking powder together into a bowl. Whisk the egg then tip into the butter and sugar with a little of the flour and beat well for 2 minutes. Add the rest of the flour, the bicarbonate of soda, the vanilla essence, the dates and the soaking water and mix well. The mixture should have the consistency of a batter.

Pour the mixture into a buttered baking tin and bake in the preheated oven for 40 minutes.

To make the sauce, heat the butter with the sugar until the sugar has dissolved. Add the cream and gently heat through, stirring all the time. Pour over the pudding and serve with good vanilla ice cream.

Jam Roly-poly

This pudding harks back to my school days, when we would all line up for lunch. The boy at the front would spot the roly-poly pudding being set out and the message would soon be sent down the line of boys like a Mexican wave.

Serves 4

- 250g/9oz self-raising flour
- 130g/4½oz suet
- ½ teaspoon salt
- 115g/4oz jam
- caster sugar for sprinkling

In a large bowl, sift the flour and mix in the suet and salt. Add enough water to make a stiff paste. Tip out on to a floured board and roll out into an oblong shape about 1.5cm/½ inch thick.

Spread with jam, then dampen the outer edges with water and roll up into a 'sausage'. Press the join firmly to seal. Wrap the roll in greaseproof or non-stick baking paper, pleating along the length of the roll to allow for expansion. Then wrap this roll in a sheet of pleated foil, ensuring that the joins are tightly sealed so that it is water-tight.

Steam for 1 hour. Alternatively, you can put the roll into a baking tin and cook it in a preheated oven at 200°C/400°F/gas mark 6 for about 40 minutes. Unwrap the pudding and cook for a further 15 minutes or until lightly browned.

Sprinkle with caster sugar and leave to cool slightly before serving.

Ginger Rice Pudding

I am a massive fan of ginger and I also love rice pudding, so it made perfect sense to put the two together.

Serves 4

- 30g/1oz butter, plus more for greasing
- 565ml/1 pint milk
- 50g/2oz vanilla caster sugar
- 50g/2oz pudding rice
- 4 tablespoons double cream
- 30g/1oz preserved stem ginger, chopped into small pieces

Preheat the oven to 170°C/325°F/gas mark 3.

Butter an ovenproof dish and put in the milk, sugar, rice, cream and ginger. Stir well, and dot little knobs of the butter all over the top. Bake in the preheated oven for about 2 hours, until the top is golden brown, taking care not to let the pudding dry out.

Bread and Butter Pudding

Bread and butter pudding is one of my mum's classics. She would make a huge batch of it and the rest of the family would be munching on it for days. This is a variation on my mum's recipe – the marmalade adds a fantastic citrus quality. You can use any marmalade for this, but lemon or lime works particularly well.

Serves 4–6

- 6 slices day-old white bread, crusts removed
- butter
- marmalade
- 3 eggs
- 50g/2oz caster sugar
- 225ml/8fl oz milk
- 60ml/2fl oz double cream
- granulated sugar for sprinkling

Make marmalade sandwiches with the bread, butter and marmalade, then butter the outside of the bread too. Cut each sandwich diagonally into four. Arrange the quarters in a medium-sized, shallow buttered ovenproof dish so they sit snugly on top of each other.

Beat the eggs and sugar together in a bowl until creamy. Mix the milk and cream together and whisk into the eggs and sugar. Pour the mixture over the bread and leave to stand for 30 minutes or so.

Meanwhile, preheat the oven to 180°C/350°F/gas mark 4. Sprinkle granulated sugar over the pudding and put the dish in a roasting tin. Pour in enough boiling water to come halfway up the side of the dish. Bake in the preheated oven for about 45 minutes, until the custard is set and the top is golden and crispy.

Steamed Treacle Pudding

This is one of those desserts that when ordered in a restaurant and brought to the table are real head-turners. When made properly it has got to be up there among the greats.

Sift the flour into a large bowl and add the suet, brown sugar, ginger, salt and bicarbonate of soda. Mix well, then add the beaten egg, golden syrup and milk.

Stir the mixture and pour into a greased 1.1 litre/2 pint pudding basin, leaving a gap of about 4–5cm/1½–2 inches at the top so that the pudding has room to rise.

Cut out a square of tinfoil to cover the basin and grease one side with butter. Place the foil, greased side down, over the top of the basin and make a pleat of about 2.5cm/1 inch across the top – this will allow for the pudding to rise and expand. Tie the foil around the rim of the basin with string – winding it twice around the basin rim, then looping it over the top to form a handle before tying it.

Place the basin in a large lidded saucepan and pour in enough boiling water to come halfway up the side of the basin. Put the lid on the pan. The water needs to be kept steadily boiling, and should be topped up with more boiling water from time to time to maintain the level.

Steam for 2 hours, then remove the basin from the saucepan and take off the foil. Run a knife around the edge of the pudding and turn out on to a large warmed plate.

Serve with cream, custard or ice cream.

Serves 4–6

- 225g/8oz plain flour
- 85g/3oz shredded suet
- 50g/2oz soft brown sugar
- 2 teaspoons ground ginger
- ¼ teaspoon salt
- 1 level teaspoon bicarbonate of soda
- 1 beaten egg
- 50g/2oz golden syrup
- 75ml/2½ fl oz milk

Ginger Beer

Ginger beer is in everyone's childhood memories – it really is the stuff of school holidays! Real ginger beer is easy to make and tastes far better than commercially made varieties. First you need to make a ginger beer 'plant' – this can be reused time and time again and makes a batch of drinks once a week. The plant is a mixture of dried ginger, yeast, sugar and water, which creates a yeast culture.

In the jar, place 1 teaspoon of dried yeast, 2 teaspoons of ground ginger, 4 teaspoons of sugar and 565ml/1 pint of cold water. Stir, then loosely replace the lid. Keep at room temperature. Every day, feed the plant with 2 teaspoons of ground ginger and 4 teaspoons of sugar, giving it a good stir afterwards. After a week, the plant will be ready and you can make the ginger beer.

To make the beer

Place 1kg/2lb 3oz of sugar and 1 litre/1¾ pints of boiling water In a large pan and stir until the sugar has dissolved. Add the juice of the 4 lemons to the pan.

Strain the contents of the ginger beer plant from the jar through a fine cloth into the pan. Put the cloth with the sediment to one side for now.

Add 7 litres/12 pints of room temperature water to the pan and stir. Using a jug and a funnel, if you have one, fill the bottles about seven-eighths full – you need to allow for expansion. Squeeze the air out of the bottles to prevent them exploding under pressure from their contents and screw on the lids.

Store the bottles in a safe place at room temperature, and leave for 3 to 4 weeks to 'brew'. This version of ginger beer is very mildly alcoholic, due to the yeast and sugar action.

The sediment in the cloth should be halved. You can discard one half of the solid from the plant or give it to someone so they may start their own plant. Place the remaining half in a clean jar with 565ml/1 pint of water and continue to feed as above. Repeat the bottling process each week as desired . . . although you may find your life becomes overtaken by ginger beer!

Each batch makes 2 litres/3½ pints

- dried yeast
- ground ginger
- sugar
- water
- juice of 4 lemons
- a jar with a lid, big enough to contain the plant
- a measuring jug
- a large pan
- a fine cloth for straining the plant
- several clean and dry 2 litre plastic bottles with screw-top lids
- a funnel to fill the bottles (optional)

Lemon Barley Water

Traditionally used as a restorative, barley water is probably more likely to be associated with tennis-racquet-wielding superstars at Wimbledon now! It is a great refresher on a hot sunny day.

Wash the barley and put it into a saucepan with sufficient water just to cover it. Boil for 3 minutes, then strain and discard the water.

Put the barley into a large heat-resistant jug with the lemon rind and the sugar. Pour over 1.1 litre/2 pints of boiling water, stir well to dissolve the sugar and leave to cool.

Once cool, add the lemon juice. Stir, strain and serve.

Makes approx. 1.1 litres/2 pints

- 115g/4oz pearl barley
- thinly pared rind of $\frac{1}{2}$ a lemon
- 50g/2oz sugar
- 1.1 litres/2 pints water
- juice of 2 lemons

Elderflower Cordial

Elderflower cordial encapsulates all that is summer. Delicious when simply diluted with sparkling water and served over ice with a slice of lemon.

First give the elderflowers heads a shake and a quick rinse under cold water to dislodge any creepy-crawlies that may be hidden among the flowers. Bring the water to the boil in a large, clean saucepan.

In a large heatproof bowl, place the sliced lemons, elderflowers, sugar and citric acid. Pour over the water as soon as it has boiled, and stir until the sugar has dissolved.

Once the liquid is cool, cover with a clean tea towel. Let the mixture steep for at least 3 or 4 days, stirring once or twice a day. It will increase in strength over time, so taste it to see if it needs further steeping. When it is ready, strain the cordial through a muslin-lined sieve and pour into very clean bottles – plastic water bottles are fine – leaving a little space at the top in case of fermentation.

Keep in the fridge and use within 2 weeks, or store in the freezer for future use. This makes such a refreshing drink mixed with 5 parts sparkling water.

Makes approx. 1.2 litres/2¼ pints

- 20 elderflower heads
- 1.2 litres/2¼ pints boiling water
- 2 lemons, sliced
- 1.5kg/3½lb sugar
- 2 teaspoons citric acid

Useful Addresses

Markets and Farm Shops

National Farmers' Retail & Markets Association (FARMA)
The Greenhouse
P.O. Box 575
Southampton SO15 7BZ
Tel: 0845 44 88 420
http://www.farma.org.uk

National Association of Farmers' Markets
P.O. Box 575
Southampton SO15 7BZ
Tel: 0845 45 88 420
http://www.farmersmarkets.net/default.htm

London Farmers' Markets
11 O'Donnell Court
Brunswick Centre
London WC1N 1NY
Tel: 020 7833 0338
http://www.lfm.org.uk/index.asp

Food Lovers' Fairs
Unit 203, Buspace Studios
Conlan Street
London W10 5AP
Tel: 020 8206 6111
http://www.foodloversbritain.com

Food from Britain
4th Floor, Manning House
22 Carlisle Place
London SW1P 1JA
Tel: 020 7233 5111
http://www.regionalfoodanddrink.co.uk/directory

Meat, Fish and Eggs

The Guild of Q Butchers
P.O. Box 26139
Dunfermline
Fife KY12 7WJ
Tel: 01383 432622
http://www.guildofqbutchers.com

Pork

The Essex Pig Company
Pannington Hall Farm
Wherstead
Ipswich IP9 2AR
Tel: 0845 95 00 210
Information@essexpigcompany.com
http://www.essexpigcompany.com

Sillfield Farm
Endmoor
Kendal
Cumbria LA8 0HZ
Tel: 01539 567609
http://www.sillfield.co.uk/index.htm

Beef

Farmhouse Direct
Long Ghyll Farms
Brock Close
Bleasdale
Preston PR3 1UZ
Tel: 01995 61799
http://www.farmhousedirect.com

Wild Beef

Hillhead Farm
Chagford
Devon TQ13 8DY
Tel: 01647 433433

Lamb

Farmer Sharp
Borough Market
8 Southwark Street
London SE1 1TL
Tel: 020 7407 1002
http://www.farmersharp.co.uk/2002/index.asp

Blackface Lamb
Weatherall Foods Limited
Crochmore House
Irongray
Dumfries DG2 9SF
Tel: 01387 730326
http://www.blackface.co.uk/scottish_blackface_lamb.asp

Poultry, Fish and Game

Furness Fish Poultry & Game Supplies
Stockbridge Lane
Dalton Gate
Ulverston
Cumbria LA12 7BG
Tel: 01229 585037

Kelly Turkey Farms
Springate Farm
Bicknacre Road
Danbury
Essex CM3 4EP
Tel: 01245 223581
http://www.kelly-turkeys.com

Sutton Hoo Chickens
Kennel Farm
Hasketon
Woodbridge
Suffolk IP13 6JX
Tel: 01394 386797

Furness Fish Poultry and Game
Stockbridge Lane
Dalton Gate
Ulverston
Cumbria LA12 7BG
Tel: 01229 585037

two fishwives
a16, Alpha Business Centre
7–11 Minerva Road
London NW10 6HJ
Tel: 020 8537 1168
http://www.twofishwives.com

Maldon Oyster & Seafood LLP
Birchwood Farm
Cock Clarks
Chelmsford
Essex CM3 6RF
Tel: 01621 828699
http://www.maldonoysters.com

The Wild Meat Company
Low Road
Sweffling
Saxmundham
Suffolk IP17 2BU
Tel: 01728 663211
http://members.farmline.com/
wildmeat

Livestock Associations

British Pig Association
Trumpington Mews
40b High Street
Trumpington
Cambridge CB2 2LS
Tel: 01223 845100
http://www.britishpigs.org.uk

National Sheep Association
The Sheep Centre
Malvern
Worcestershire WR13 6PH
Tel: 01684 892661
http://www.nationalsheep.org.uk

National Beef Association
Mart Centre
Tyne Green
Hexham
Northumberland NE46 3SG
Tel: 01434 601005
http://www.nationalbeef
association.co.uk

British Poultry Council
Europoint House
5 Lavington Street
London SE1 0NZ
Tel: 020 7202 4760
http://www.poultry.uk.com/main.
htm

Hatch-It Incubators
Palady Spring
Old Andover Road
Newbury RG20 0LS
Tel: 01635 230238
www.hatchitincubators.com

Pantry Products, Vegetables,
Herbs and Seeds

Jules & Sharpie LaLa Limited
2b & 2c Eastlands Road
Leiston
Suffolk IP16 4LL
Tel: 01728 833955
http://www.julesandsharpie.com

Jekka's Herb Farm
Tel: 01454 418878
http://www.jekkasherbfarm.com

Seeds of Italy
Phoenix Industrial Estate
Rosslyn Crescent
Harrow
Middlesex HA1 2SP
Tel: 020 8427 5020
http://www.seedsofitaly.sagenet.
co.uk/default.htm

Mrs Tee's Wild Mushrooms
Gorse Meadow
Sway Road
Lymington
Hampshire SO41 8LR
Tel: 01590 673354
www.wildmushrooms.co.uk

Useful Organizations

**DEFRA (Department for
Environment, Food and
Rural Affairs)**
Information Resource Centre
Lower Ground Floor
Ergon House
c/o Nobel House
17 Smith Square
London SW1P 3JR
Tel: 0845 93 35 577
http://www.defra.gov.uk

Soil Association
Bristol House
40–56 Victoria Street
Bristol BS1 6BY
Tel: 01173 145000
http://www.soilassociation.org/
web/sa/saweb.nsf

**Garden Organic
(formerly HDRA)**
Ryton Organic Gardens
Coventry
Warwickshire CV8 3LG
Tel: 02476 303517
http://www.gardenorganic.org.uk

The Ramblers' Association
FREEPOST SW15
London SE1 7BR
Tel: 020 7339 8500
http://www.ramblers.org.uk

RSPCA Freedom Foods
http://www.rspca.org.uk

Rare Breeds Survival Trust
Stoneleigh Park
Warwickshire CV8 2LG
Tel: 02476 696551
http://www.rbst.org.uk

Index

allotments 222
anytime marmalade 277
aphids 196
apples
    apple and elderberry pie 251
    apple and sage jelly 279
    dried 289
apricots, dried 288
aromatic oil with wild garlic 92

bacon
    cabbage with onion and bacon 238
    dandelion and bacon salad 96–7
    hawthorn bud and bacon
        pudding 98
    liver and bacon 40–41
    mini pigs in blankets 163
    rosemary kebabs 182–3
baked oranges in rum 172–3
baked trout in cider-soaked
        newspaper 154
bananas and vanilla sugar 174–5
bantams 69
barbecuing 179–83
Barnsley chops 39
basil
    growing 219
    Uncle Max's chunky pesto 239
bath herbs 243
beans
    growing 211, 224
    spiced green beans 287
    storing 258
beef
    all in one can of beer stew 55
    boiled beef and carrots 54
    cuts 51–3
    farming 48–51
beef steak fungus 123
beer, all in one can of beer stew 55
bins, keeping fresh 264
biological pest control 195
bird droppings, cleaning 266
blackberries 120
    blackberry junket 131
blackcurrants 217
boiled beef and carrots 54
boiled goose egg with chunky
        soldiers 72

boots, taking care of 264
borage 100, 242
bottling 131, 280–3
braised pigeon 142–3
brassicas 208–9
bread
    bread and butter pudding 308–9
    brown bread ice cream 76–7
    keeping fresh 262
broad beans 211
broccoli 208
Brussels sprouts 208
bulb crops 212, 213
butchers 23
butter beans 258

cabbage
    cabbage with onion and bacon 238
    growing 208
    sausages and ham with
        red cabbage 28–9
cabbage white butterfly 208
Camembert, foil-baked 168, 169
campfire 147–8
    boiling water over 178
    building 148–9, 152
    cooking over 152–3
    fuel 150
candied chestnuts 126–7
carrot root fly 196, 213
carrots
    boiled beef and carrots 54
    carrot and coriander soup 228
    growing 196, 212, 213
Catherine wheel sausages 176–7
chamomile
    as bath herb 243
    tea 244, 264
charcoal 179
chard 209
cheese
    Caela's cheesy chilli sticks 293
    foil-baked Camembert 168, 169
    rosemary kebabs 182–3
cherries in brandy 250
chestnut see sweet chestnut
chicken
    buying 62–3
    chicken sandwich 64–5
    chicken stock 67
    spicy chicken supper 66
    whole roast chicken with

rosemary and thyme butter
        156–7
chickens
    broiler production systems 62–3
    buying 59
    and family pets 60
    and foxes 60
    free-range 62, 63
    housing and feeding 60, 91
    keeping 56–62
    need for cockerels 62
chickweed 91
chilli
    Caela's cheesy chilli sticks 293
    flakes 259
    oil 259
    sweet chilli jam 276
chives 196, 219
chrysanthemum 213
chutney, tomato 290–1
cider
    baked trout in cider-soaked
        newspaper 154
    pears poached in cider 246–7
    pot roast pork fillet with nettle
        stuffing and cider and cream
        sauce 94–5
cleaning
    bird droppings 266
    burnt irons 267
    frying pans 266
    glass 266
    stained metal 266
    vases 267
    wax 267
cloves 259
cockerels 62
cold tea polish 267
comfrey 202
companion planting 196, 213
compost 202–3
coriander
    carrot and coriander soup 228
    seeds 259
cos lettuce 206
countryside code 84
courgettes 214
crab apples 100
    jelly 278
    spiced crab-apples 115
crisphead lettuce 206
crisps, root vegetable 234–5

custard
  custard sauce 75
  Italian warm custard 75
cut and come again lettuce 206

dandelion 91
  dandelion and bacon salad 96–7
deer 133
Dijon mustard 258
dogs
  and chickens 60
  in the countryside 84
drying food 288–9
duck 137
  duck with figs 138–9
  eggs 71
dustbin oven 184–5, 187

eel 165
eggs 69–71
  barn 70
  battery system 70
  boiled goose egg with chunky
    soldiers 72
  custard sauce 75
  duck 71
  enriched cage system 70
  free-range 70
  goose 71
  homemade mayonnaise 74
  Italian warm custard 75
  ostrich 71
  quails' 71
  spinach omelette 73
elder 103
  apple and elderberry pie 251
  as bath herb 243
  elderflower cordial 313
  elderflower fritters 118–19
  preserved elderberries 131

farm shops 23
farmers' markets 23
farming 14–17
fat
  on meat 14, 16
  pork 20, 22
  in soups/stews 263
fat hen 91
fennel
  sea bass with wild fennel 108–9
  seeds 120, 259
  wild 104, 108–9

fertilizers 78, 200–3
field mushrooms 123
  dried 289
fillet steak 52
fire, in the countryside 84
firewood
  collection 150
  slow/fast burning 150
  storage 150
fish on boards 166–7
foil-baked Camembert 168, 169
foxes 60
French beans 211
  spiced green beans 287
frying pans
  choosing 260
  cleaning 266
fungi
  beef steak fungus 123
  dried mushrooms 289
  field mushroom 123
  Jew's ears 104
  parasol mushroom 104
  puffball 91
  wild mushrooms on toast 124–5

game 132–7
gardening 190–3
  in containers 222–5
  feeding and watering plants
    198–203
  herbs 218–21
  pest control 194–7
  soft fruit 216–17
  vegetables 204–15
gazpacho 226–7
geese
  boiled goose egg with chunky
    soldiers 72
  eggs 71, 72
  feeding 91
gin 123
  sloe gin 128–9
ginger 259
  ginger beer 312
  ginger rice pudding 306–7
  gingerbread pigs 294–5
glass, cleaning 266
goat's cheese, rosemary kebabs
    182–3
grapes 216
gravy

  smooth 263
  traditional 46
green beans see French beans
  greens 208–9
gumbo 133

ham
  baked ham 34–5
  sausages and ham with
    red cabbage 28–9
hanging baskets 223
hangover cure 264
hare 133
haws 103
hawthorn 91, 103
  hawthorn bud and bacon
    pudding 98
  hawthorn flower liqueur 99
hazel
  nuts 120
  walking-sticks 89
herbs 218–21
  bags 269
  for the bath 243
  container growing 224
  dried 259
  drying 289
  ice cubes 242
  oils 259
  pot-pourri 269
  teas 244–5
herring, fish on boards 166–7
hock 25
hog roast 158
hogget 38
holly, frosted leaves 269
honey 258
  lavender and honey lamb 230–31
horseradish 103
  sauce 110–11

ice cream, brown bread 76–7
iceberg lettuce 206
intensive farming 16, 19, 20, 78
irons, cleaning 267
Italian warm custard 75

jam pans 271
jam roly-poly 305
jams and jellies 270–9
  apple and sage jelly 279
  crab-apple jelly 278
  strawberry jam 274–5

sweet chilli jam 276
very easy raspberry jam 275
Jerusalem artichoke 212
Jew's ears 104
juniper 123
berries 259

kale 209
kettle, descaling 267
kindling 152
knives
kitchen 261
sharpening 261

lamb
cuts 38–9
farming 37–8
Lancashire hotpot 46–7
lavender and honey lamb 230–31
liver and bacon 40–41
shepherd's pie 42–3
squab pie 44
Lancashire hotpot 46–7
larder 257–9
lavender
bags 269
as bath herb 243
biscuits 248–9
lavender and honey lamb 230–31
leeks
growing 212
potato and leek bake 232–3
lemon balm 242
lemon verbena 242
lemons
juice 263
lemon barley water 313
lemon curd 302–3
skins 264
lettuce
growing 196, 206, 224
varieties 206
lids, releasing 264
lime flowers (linden)
as bath herb 243
tea 103, 244
liqueur
hawthorn berry 103
hawthorn flower 99
liquid manure 202
liver and bacon 40–41
liver fluke 207
loose leaf lettuce 206

mackerel, fish on boards 166–7
mallard 137
manure 200
liquid 202
marigold 243
marmalade, anytime 277
marrows
growing 214
marrow stuffed with
sausagemeat 170–71
tomato and onion marrow 236–7
mayonnaise, homemade 74
meat, tenderizing 263
metal, cleaning 266
milk production 48, 50
mince, bulking out 263
mint
easy peasy pea and mint soup 229
growing 220
ice cubes 242
sauce 240–241
tea 244
water mint 104
muffins 296–7
Muscovy duck 138
mushrooms see fungi
mussels cooked in a sack 155
mustard 258
mutton 38

nasturtium 207
nettles 90
in fertilizer 202
pot roast pork fillet with nettle
stuffing and cider and
cream sauce 94–5

oils 259
aromatic oil with wild garlic 92
olive oil 259
omelette, spinach 73
onions 212
cabbage with onion and bacon 238
peeling 263
pickled 286
salad/spring 213
tomato and onion marrow 236–7
orach 208
oranges
baked oranges in rum 172–3
pomanders 269
ostrich eggs 71
outdoor life 144–89

pans 260
jam-making 271
paprika 259
parasol mushroom 104
parsley 220
parsnips 212
partridge 135
pasta 259
peaches
bottled 283
dried 288
pears
dried 289
pears poached in cider 246–7
peas
easy peasy pea and mint soup 229
growing 211, 224
pectin 271
peppers
growing 224
sweet pickled peppers 284–5
pest control 196
natural/biological 195
pesticides 78, 83
pesto, Uncle Max's chunky 239
pheasant 135
pheasant with red wine and
raisins 140
pickled onions 286
pickling 284–7
pig farming 19–20
pigeon 46, 137
braised pigeon 142–3
pit bake 185
plants
feeding 199, 200–3
sun exposure 199
watering 199
plums, dried 288
polish, cold tea 267
pomanders 269
poppy 120
pork
baked ham 34–5
buying 23
cabbage with onion and bacon 238
crackling 24
cuts 24–5
dandelion and bacon salad 96–7
farming methods 19–20
fat 20, 22

flavour 22
marrow stuffed with sausagemeat 170–71
mini pigs in blankets 163
pork scratchings 31
pot roast pork fillet with nettle stuffing and cider and cream sauce 94–5
rillettes 33
roast 30
sausages and ham with red cabbage 28–9
spit-roasted barbecued rack of sticky ribs 162
toad in the hole 26–7
pot-pourri 269
potatoes
    growing 212, 224
    potato and leek bake 232–3
pots
    for growing vegetables 223
    kitchen 260
prawns on sticks 164–5
preserved elderberries 131
preserving 131, 254–91
primitive breeds 37, 38
puddings
    Aunt Thelma's easiest sticky toffee pudding 304
    bread and butter pudding 308–9
    ginger rice pudding 306–7
    jam roly poly 305
    steamed treacle pudding 310–11
puffball 91
pulses 258
pumpkin 214
pyrethrin 213

quails' eggs 71

rabbits 132–3
    deterring 214
    'Kentucky fried' rabbit 141
ramsons see wild garlic
rapeseed oil 259
Rare Breeds Survival Trust 23
rare/traditional breeds 11, 14, 16–17, 23
raspberries, very easy raspberry jam 275
red cabbage, sausages and ham with red cabbage 28–9
red clover 100
rhubarb and strawberry crumble 252–3
rice 259
    ginger rice pudding 306–7
roasting trays 260
rocket 206–7, 223, 224
root crops 212, 213
root vegetable crisps 234–5
rose, wild/dog 123
rosehips 123
rosemary
    growing 220
    rosemary kebabs 182–3
    tea 244, 264
    trout with rosemary 107
    whole roast chicken with rosemary and thyme butter 156–7
rum, baked oranges in rum 172–3
rump steak 53
runner beans 211

sabayon 75
sage 219
    apple and sage jelly 279
salads
    container growing 224
    dandelion and bacon salad 96–7
    growing 206–7
salmon, spit-roasted stuffed salmon 160–61
salt 258
    on boots/shoes 264
    over-salted food 263
    salt and pepper seasoning 262
samphire 112–13
sardines, fish on boards 166–7
sausages
    Catherine wheel sausages 176–7
    marrow stuffed with sausagemeat 170–71
    rosemary kebabs 182–3
    sausages and ham with red cabbage 28–9
    toad in the hole 26–7
sea bass with wild fennel 108–9
sea salt 258
seakale beet 209
seed potatoes 212
self-sufficiency 12, 193, 216
Seymour, John 12, 216
sheep
    farming 37–8
    Jacob 37
    Soay 37, 38
    see also lamb
shepherd's pie 42–3
shin beef 53
silverside 53
sirloin steak 51
sleeplessness 264
sloe gin 128–9
slugs 196
smoking 186
    cold 186, 188
    hot 188, 189
snails 196
soft fruit 216–17
    see also preserving
soups
    carrot and coriander soup 228
    easy peasy pea and mint soup 229
    gazpacho 226–7
spiced green beans 287
spicy chicken supper 66
spinach 91
    growing 207
    omelette 73
spit-roasting 158
    barbecued rack of sticky ribs 162
    stuffed salmon 160–61
sprouting broccoli 208
squab pie 44
squirrel 133
steamed treacle pudding 310–11
sticky ribs, spit-roasted barbecued rack of sticky ribs 162
sticky toffee pudding, Aunt Thelma's easiest 304
stinging nettles see nettles
stock
    chicken 67
    rich 263
stockman's hock 25
strawberries
    container growing 224
    growing 217
    jam 274–5
    rhubarb and strawberry crumble 252–3
    wild 104, 105, 217
    wild strawberry syllabub 116–17
Suffolk cakes 298–9
sugar
    syrup 280
    vanilla 174

swede 212
sweet chestnut 123
   candied chestnuts 126–7
sweet chilli jam 276
sweet pickled peppers 284–5
sweetcorn
   growing 214
   sweetcorn in their jackets 180, 181

T-bone steak 52
   barbecued 180
tea, cold tea polish 267
tea bread 300–301
teal 137
teapots, keeping fresh 262
tenderizing meat 263
thumb stick 89
thyme 219
   as bath herb 243
   tea 244
   whole roast chicken with rosemary and thyme butter 156–7

toad in the hole 26–7
tomatoes
   growing 214, 224
   tomato chutney 290–91
   tomato and onion marrow 236–7
topside 53
Traditional Breeds Meat Marketing scheme 23
treacle pudding, steamed 310–11
trotters 25
trout
   baked trout in cider-soaked newspaper 154
   trout with rosemary 107
turkeys 63
turnips 212

Uncle Max's chunky pesto 239

vanilla sugar 174
vases, cleaning 267
vegetables
   growing 204–15
   keeping fresh 262
   see also preserving

venison 133
vinegars 259
   wild garlic 92

walking-sticks 87, 88–9
water, boiling over a campfire 178
water mint 104
watercress 207
watering 199
wax, cleaning 267
widgeon 137
wild boar 22
wild garlic 90
   aromatic oil with wild garlic 92
   vinegar 92
wild meat 132–7
wild mushrooms on toast 124–5
wild rocket 207
window-boxes 223
wood pigeon see pigeon

zabaglione 75

Big thanks to:

Nikki for all her hard work and patience – without you this book would never have been possible. A massive thank you to Chris for his amazing photos and rubbish jokes and to Camilla for believing in the whole project from the beginning, as well as drinking all my wine! Thanks to John for pulling everything together with your special magic.

Thanks to Debbie at Fresh for keeping me on the right track and Henry the Toff for being a great friend. A very special thanks to everyone at the farm for working so hard over the last year and making the Essex Pig Company what it is today. Also big cheers to Dolly, Animal Mark and everyone at Harlow City Farm and Colchester Zoo. To Paul Kelly, you are nuts, but you do produce the best turkey in the world.

Thank you to all my great mates: Marc Cooper for all the laughter, Simon and Luciana for the best Sunday nights, Matt, Carly, Simon and Hayley for all the good times, not forgetting Saffy. To Andy, Jum,

Jools and the kids, to Sue and Steve – thanks for all your love and support over the years. To Anna for eating all of my salami, you will find your Maynard some day. To the lovely Asa, you are a legend but I'm still coming round to get all of my cookbooks back! Thanks to Dan Snow for the long conversations about the great battles of World War Two. To Peter Gott and Vaughan Byrne a massive thank you for sharing your vast wisdom and knowledge with me.

To my Mum, Dad and brother Danny for always being there and giving me such a great childhood. To my wonderful partner Michaela: you are my life and love, you give me the strength to carry on, but how you put up with all my crazy ideas I will never know.

Thanks as well to all at Penguin who worked around the clock to make this book happen: Sarah Fraser, Sarah Hulbert, Tiina Wastie, Helen Eka, Chantal Gibbs, Annie Lee, and Sarah Tildesley and all her posh assistants.

acknowledgements